SAVING STRAITSMOUTH ISLAND

SAVING STRAITSMOUTH ISLAND

A HISTORY

PAUL ST. GERMAIN

THE History PRESS

Published by The History Press
Charleston, SC
www.historypress.com

Cover images: Top image is Straitsmouth Lighthouse and both keeper houses from 1835 and 1878, including the milking barn on the far right, circa 1890. *Courtesy of Sandy Bay Historical Society*. Bottom image is an aerial view of Straitsmouth Island taken from a drone. *Courtesy of Vincent Nappa, 2016.*

First published 2020

Manufactured in the United States

ISBN 9781467145077

Library of Congress Control Number: 2020930474

This book is dedicated to the volunteers of the Thacher Island Association past, present and future and especially the "Straitsmouth Savages," who have endured the sun, rain, ticks and poison ivy on the island for the past nine years. Their work has resulted in the total restoration of this National Historic Register site that is now enjoyed by the public for the first time in 180 years.

CONTENTS

PREFACE

In 2010, the Town of Rockport took ownership of 1.8 acres of land at the eastern end of Straitsmouth Island as well as the 1896 lighthouse tower. The plan was to partner the Thacher/Straitsmouth Island Town Committee (T/SITC) with the volunteers of the Thacher Island Association (TIA) to begin the restoration process of the island and its various historic structures. TIA has had this same arrangement on Thacher Island since 1980. While T/SITC manages the islands, TIA raises the funds for their restoration and maintenance.

It was at this juncture that I felt obliged to do some basic research on the island, as I had done on Thacher in 1999. The Thacher research resulted in the nomination and eventually the naming of the Cape Ann Light Station on Thacher as a National Historic Landmark by the National Park Service in 2001. NHL designation is only awarded to historic places that hold exceptional national significance because of their abilities to illustrate U.S. heritage. Only 2,600 NHLs are in existence today. Thacher has joined the ranks of such famous sites as Yosemite National Park, the Grand Canyon, the Lincoln Memorial and the USS *Constitution*.

While conducting my research on Straitsmouth, I was surprised how little information was readily available. In fact, there was never a book published about Straitsmouth as there had been about Thacher, written by Rockport author Eleanor Parsons in 1984. Because Straitsmouth was listed in the National Register of Historic Places on June 15, 1987, this provided an additional reason for the entire history of this historically significant light station to be more completely documented.

My objective has been to record as much history as I could find in the hopes that future generations might learn about how Straitsmouth Island fit into the growth of Cape Ann and the role it played in saving the lives and the vessels of mariners both local and distant.

THIS IS THE FIFTH book I've written about the historical sites and people of Cape Ann. It seems that each book followed a similar pattern. Starting with a visit to the Sandy Bay Historical Society and its archives. Once again, I started there to learn more about the people and the places surrounding Straitsmouth Island. Gwen Stevenson, the director, was her usual helpful and knowledgeable self. She first directed me to the Ebenezer Pool Papers, which several historians often relied on in their books going back to the 1860s. She also directed me to the many genealogical records and family trees of the first families of Rockport. In addition, she showed me the fine collection of Indian relics. Reviewing these stone implements, plummet stones and Indian arrowheads, I came across some papers written by Mary Ellen Lepionka, an accomplished anthropologist who has done significant research on the Indians of Cape Ann and the surrounding towns. After reading several of her papers, I contacted her, and we had wonderful and informative discussions via e-mail. She not only answered my questions but also provided more relevant information on the Indians who once gathered around Straitsmouth Point and Gap Head. Her knowledge of the Indian population was quite astonishing. She generously agreed to allow me to use much of her information in this book, and for this, I thank her.

I also want to thank Les Bartlett, a local historian with a vast knowledge of the granite quarry business on Cape Ann. His collection of vintage photographs was also helpful in identifying particular people and locations around Rockport.

I must thank Sharron Cohen, a volunteer worker in the Thacher Island Association, who was gracious enough to offer to do some genealogical research work on the sixteen lighthouse keepers stationed on the island from 1835 until 1933. Sharron has been an important contributor to the association's biannual newsletter. If anybody knows "where the bodies are buried," it would be Sharron. She's familiar with Cape Ann burying grounds and loves to dig in to find intimate details from a wide variety of sources. Most of the information in the ninth chapter about the keepers was developed, researched and written by Sharron.

In my chapter on shipwrecks occurring near Straitsmouth Island, I must thank Captain Raymond H. Bates Jr., who allowed me to use a few stories from his recent book, *Shipwrecks North of Boston Volume II: Cape Ann.* His generosity was helpful in illustrating just how dangerous the shoals' ledges and reefs surrounding Straitsmouth Island can be, even today.

The staff at the Cape Ann Museum was helpful in finding not only digital images but also information from people such as Erik Ronnberg Jr., maritime curator, who briefed me on the many interesting little-known facts about the early fishing industry of Cape Ann. Martha Oaks, museum curator, permitted me to use many of the images, and Leon Doucette, curatorial assistant, actually found the photos I was looking for and more to boot. Thank you all.

I also thank Candice Clifford, maritime historian, who helped retrieve many essential documents from the National Archives and Records Administration. In the past few years, she had found amazing amounts of information about Straitsmouth Island and its keepers in the form of documents, letter books and communications among the U.S. Lighthouse Service, the U.S. Lighthouse Establishment and the U.S. Coast Guard (USCG). I was lucky enough to be able to thank her personally before she died in 2018. Also, thanks to contributors from the U.S. Lighthouse Society, including Tom Tag, Jeff Gales and Jeremy D'Entremont, who provided keeper lists, photographs and light station information.

My friend Jonathan Strong is an author and professor of English at Tufts University and earlier at Harvard University. His fifty years correcting English papers and writing several books made him the perfect person to make amazing suggestions as to content and flow, as well as significantly "tightening up the book." Thank you, Jon.

Thanks to History Press folks Mike Kinsella, who guided me through the process and answered all my queries in a timely and professional manner, and Ryan Finn, who caught every one of my spelling inconsistencies and helped clarify the complicated family member relationships as well as eliminate duplicated entries, making the book eminently more readable.

Finally, a big thanks to my wife, Betty Ann, an author herself, for reading my manuscript and telling me what was good and bad about it, what was boring and what was interesting. Thanks, BA!

Author's note: Most of the images in this volume appear courtesy of the Sandy Bay Historical Society (SBHS), Cape Ann Museum (CAM), U.S. Coast Guard (USCG), U.S. Coast Guard Historian's Office (USCGHO) and U.S. Lighthouse Society (USLHS) and may be credited with such abbreviations.

INTRODUCTION

This book is titled *Saving Straitsmouth Island* for two reasons. The island needs to be saved in two specific ways: first by documenting its rich history and second by saving its physical infrastructure. Over the one thousand years of Straitsmouth Island's known history, it has experienced a series of "ages" or "periods," as noted in the chapter headings of the table of contents.

First and foremost, the entire history of Straitsmouth has never been documented in one place. There has never been a book published that focused solely on the Straitsmouth story. As I traced the history of Cape Ann, I found a variety of disconnected pieces of information about the island, but nothing that dealt with its entire history. I learned that Straitsmouth is not just an island but also a neighborhood adjacent to the island on the mainland.

Straitsmouth's history traces back to AD 1004, when Vikings may have walked here. Indians came here each summer to fish and hunt and dig clams. They cleared the land down to the shoreline and planted crops of corn, pumpkins, squash and beans.

John Cabot, an Italian in the employ of Henry VII of England, sailed along the coast of Massachusetts in 1498 in his search of the Northwest Passage. He undoubtedly passed the island. Samuel de Champlain, the famed French explorer of Canada, charted the coastline from Canada to Cape Cod on the second of his eleven voyages from 1604 to 1606. He met a group of Indians at Whale Cove a few hundred yards south of Straitsmouth Island to ask for their help in finding safe passage around the Cape. He named the area *Cape Aux Iles*, meaning Cape of Islands. In 1614, Captain John Smith, a founder of Jamestown, mapped the area from Penobscot Bay to Cape Cod and named the area New England. He, too, noted the island as one of three he named the three Turks Heads.

The island went through a succession of events beginning with the many explorers who noted it, passed by it or charted it. Eventually, it became a focal point for fishermen from the Chebacco area of Essex to build their fishing stages, drying fish for shipment to foreign lands. The area behind the island was for many years called Straitsmouth Point, where many of Rockport's and then Sandy Bay's first settlers set their homesteads.

The woods in the hills surrounding the island provided plentiful amounts of timber for shipbuilding and wharf construction, including pine, oak, birch, hemlock and maple.

Pirates and privateers were frequent visitors, either hiding in the area or traveling by on their questionable and often illegal missions, many times attacking vessels within sight of the island.

When fishing took hold as the major industry in 1780s, the need for navigational aids became apparent. The first lighthouses appeared with the twin lights of Thacher Island in 1771, Annisquam Light in 1801 and Straitsmouth Light, built in 1835. From 1835 until 1896, three lighthouses were built on Straitsmouth to guide mariners, fishermen and the stone sloops that carried granite from the more than fifty granite quarries dotting the area around Rockport and Annisquam.

These lights were tended by no fewer than sixteen lighthouse keepers and their families over the one hundred years until 1937. Each keeper had his own unique story.

By 1940, the USCG had little use for the island but still needed to maintain the light as an official aid to navigation. It moved its crews off the island and into the nearby U.S. Life-Saving Station at Gap Cove (sometimes called Straitsmouth Cove or Straitsmouth Life-Saving Station). The federal government sold the island in 1941 to the first of many individuals. From 1941 until 1967, it was owned by a series of private parties, the last being the Mass Audubon Society, which has maintained the 30.0-acre island as a wildlife sanctuary. In 2010, the federal government gave Rockport the lighthouse and the 1.8 acres of land it sits on, with the town's promise to maintain it in perpetuity. Rockport and Mass Audubon have since entered a cooperative agreement to manage and fully restore the historic structures, as well as build additional infrastructure that would allow the public to land safely and visit the island for the first time in more than 180 years.

I hope you enjoy reading about this small but very historic site and the people who were part of its history.

Chapter 1

VIKINGS AND INDIANS, 1004–1750

VIKINGS

"The chances are that Vikings never visited Cape Ann." So, states Mary Ellen Lepionka of Gloucester, an independent researcher who studied the prehistory of Cape Ann in preparation for a book. She is an author, editor and college instructor with a master's degree in anthropology from Boston University and postgraduate work at the University of British Columbia. She participated in salvage archaeology digs in this country, Africa and Saudi Arabia. She has written papers on Cape Ann prehistory with the Massachusetts Archaeological Society. According to Lepionka, who has done significant research on both the Vikings and Indians around Cape Ann, "I found no evidence, not even a shred of circumstantial evidence, that Leif Erikson's brother Thorvald was buried on Cape Ann in 1004 AD or even that Vikings actually set foot here. The surname actually was Eirikssen, and the father of Leif, Thorvald, and Thorstein Eirikssen was Erik Thorvaldson, or Erik the Red, the developer, if not discoverer, of Greenland."

Surviving Viking maps of the North Atlantic rim extend no farther south than fifty degrees north latitude, supporting the conclusion that the lands and peoples the Norse described may have included Algonquin but were all north of Cape Ann, which lies below the 43rd parallel. Even assuming the explorers sailed farther south than their maps record, there is a lack of accepted or substantiated evidence.

Lepionka further stated:

> *The local historical canon is inaccurate and often misleading. The official history is based largely on the works of Victorian Era historians (e.g., Thornton, 1854; Babson, 1860; Hurd, 1888; Pringle, 1892; and others) and contains contradictory timelines, factual errors, curious omissions, and debatable interpretations. Those stories have been repeated, conflated, and compounded over the generations and, where there is any awareness at all, seem to have set like concrete in the collective mind. This is too bad but not surprising. National, ethnic, civic, class, political, religious, intellectual, and personal pride or conviction are known to have distorted historical interpretations in all times and places. The story of Cape Ann is no exception.*

When the Viking Thorvald was fatally wounded by natives he had attacked, he requested to be buried at Krossanes, "Cape of the Crosses." This burial site has been claimed by Hampton, New Hampshire (which has a rock with rune-like scratchings claimed to be Thorvald's headstone), as well as by Cape Neddick, Maine; Gloucester, Massachusetts; Boston; Nahant; Lynn; and Duxbury. Duxbury even named a promontory Krossanes, quoting the same words other towns use to justify their claims. Other supposed runestones in New England—such as Dighton Rock in Berkeley, Massachusetts, on the Taunton River—have not been authenticated despite perennial speculation. In Massachusetts, artifacts or sites of proposed but disputed Norse origin have also been found in Cambridge, Hingham, Medford and several spots on Cape Cod.

The Viking craze was exploited during the 1890 Columbian Exposition in Chicago, when a replica of Leif Erikson's Viking ship was exhibited there. Historians of Cape Ann in the 1890s were not immune to the excitement. For the first time, the Vikings were added to local history. (James Robert Pringle, a journalist, publicist and amateur historian living in Gloucester at the time, likely was influenced by the Viking craze.) Pringle, citing the eleventh-century Icelandic sagas in his 1892 self-published *History of the Town and City of Gloucester, Cape Ann*, said that the Vikings named New England Vinland in 1007, but candidates for that name range from sites in Newfoundland to New Brunswick; Newport, Rhode Island; Martha's Vineyard; as far south as Virginia; and as far west as Minnesota.

In *History of the Town and City of Gloucester, Cape Ann*, Pringle wrote that Thorvald was buried in Gloucester somewhere along the Back Shore. Earlier

A replica of Leif Erikson's Viking ship was displayed at the Columbian Exposition in 1890. *Library of Congress.*

historians Adams, Babson and Thornton had somehow failed to mention this. Norse literature states that Thorvald, sailing south in AD 1004, had been going east around a rocky north-facing cape when he put ashore to mend a damaged rudder, found six Skraelings (natives) hiding under their beached canoes, killed them (except for one escapee) and was soon after mortally wounded in a retaliatory attack. It is written that he requested to be taken to a preferred spot to be buried and that the place be called Krossanes. According to Pringle, Krossanes was at Bass Rocks in Gloucester. There was even a 175-room Hotel Thorwald at Bass Rocks between 1899 and 1965, at which time it burned down.

A postage stamp issued in the United States in 1925 commemorates the Viking ship featured in the Columbian Exposition. In 1919, the Scandinavian Fraternity of America petitioned Congress to declare officially that Leif Erikson discovered North America. Ultimately, in 1964, October 9 became

Leif Erikson Day as an optional holiday and alternative to Columbus Day on the national calendar. A Leif Erikson postage stamp was issued in 1968. Appropriation of the Vikings as a cultural icon includes statues and sports teams in communities as near as Rockport, Massachusetts, and as far away as New Zealand with historically high populations of Scandinavian immigrants. In Rockport today, the local high school sports teams call themselves the Vikings.

INDIANS

Mary Ellen Lepionka published a paper in the fall 2013 Massachusetts Archaeological Society bulletin about Cape Ann prehistory in which she reviewed the works of several archaeologists, including N. Carlton Phillips, Marshall Saville, Frank Speck and Fredrick Johnson. I have summarized some of her more interesting findings about Indian life on Cape Ann.

N. Carlton Phillips (1879–1952) was president of the Russia Cement Company manufacturers of LePage's Glue in West Gloucester and was an amateur archaeologist and collector. Phillips gave unpublished drafts on archaeological sites he excavated on Cape Ann. Those papers are now in the library of the Cape Ann Museum. These papers, along with those of Marshall Saville at the Sandy Bay Historical Society, make up significant collections of Indian artifacts and history around Cape Ann. Phillips conjectured that based on bones exhumed, he felt that Indians only sought seasonal occupation of Cape Ann. He stated in his report from 1940:

> *The Indians have come here in the summertime. They didn't live here all year round. How do we know this? Well, if the Indians came here to live all year round, we would have found the whole skeleton of a bear or some such animal. But we didn't. We have only a few bones of the bear in a big shell heap, which would rather indicate that in the Spring when they came here, they had some meat on hand, and they brought it with them. Now without doubt the Indians came to Cape Ann in the summertime for purposes of getting clams and fish, which they smoked and dried and carried inland for the winter.*

The remoteness of Cape Ann, which is almost cut off from the mainland, mitigated against the Indians living in the area year-round. They confined themselves chiefly to the interior, where deep woods for camping and hunting, good soil for planting and ponds for fishing made the shore along the ocean less desirable.

Ebenezer Pool recorded his grandfather's recollections in 1823 of his witnessing the Indians; they are now housed at the Sandy Bay Historical Society museum: "[T]here were 30 to 40 wigwams in Riverview north of Pole Hill when the English began to settle Gloucester in the late 1630s. This would have constituted a sizable village. His account further asserts that the first English settlement was rented or bought land from the Pawtucket in installments in exchange for bushels of Indian corn, with only the final installment paid in cash to Samuel English in 1701, which Gloucester ironically had to sell some land to raise."

In addition to the anecdotal accounts, there is a letter from Reverend John White noting that the Dorchester Company managed to pay off debts for its failed Cape Ann fishing venture of 1623 within three years through trade with the Indians at Naumkeag (Salem) and at Fisherman's Field, which is today's Stage Fort Park in Gloucester. Town records seldom refer to Indians except to report mischief or fears of uprisings or laws relating to them enacted by the General Court of Massachusetts Bay Colony.

Various writings have indicated that Indian names such as Pawtucket, Pennacook, Agawam and Abenaki were often confused with tribal names and/or locations. The Native Americans who lived on Cape Ann most recently were known as the Pawtucket but were also called the Agawam and the Wamesit by colonists and early historians. All three names refer to places (villages) rather than to people or territories, however, and they were all the same people. Confusion over group names arose partly because the Algonquin of New England usually referred to themselves simply as belonging to a village or as "the People" or "the Real/Original People" of whatever place or landscape they were in at a given time. Place names usually were not unique but could apply to any location where the landscape had the same geographic or ecological features. There are other places called Agawam and Pawtucket, for example. Another source of confusion in Algonquin place names is European observers' mistakes in hearing, transcribing and translating the words.

The English settlers who encountered the Pawtucket in Ipswich, Essex and Cape Ann in the summers called them the Agawam Indians, a term still used today. Agawam is also a place name on colonial maps for an area that encompasses Gloucester and Rockport and the rest of eastern Essex County. The last recorded Contact-era sagamore of Agawam, whom the colonists called Masconomet or Masconomo and later Sagamore John, and his descendants signed over the deeds to these towns.

In Ms. Lepionka's work, she often refers to the "Contact Period," which is defined as the period of European contact prior to settlement. In New England, the Contact Period runs for about one hundred years from 1540 to 1640. Coastal native people were familiar with Europeans long before the Pilgrims landed. Some, such as the Abenaki sagamore Samoset, had even learned English from seasonal fishermen on the Maine coast who came from Europe.

In an interview with Ms. Lepionka, she told me, "Native people were fishing at Gap Head and exploiting the rookeries on Straitsmouth Island and Milk Island as well as Thacher's. Exploiting the rookeries entailed hunting fowl and gathering eggs (a delicacy), as well as feathers for decorative wear. A cache of Late Archaic Period stone plummets and grooved surf net weights was found in Land's End by Marshall Saville in the 1920s." (A plummet is a stone artifact resembling a carpenter's plumb bob, usually made of basalt, slate or hematite. Marked by a single groove around it toward one end or the middle, it was possibly a sinker for fishing or of ceremonial or ritual use.)

"The native people likely were netting shoal fish, such as striped bass, crossing the bar between Land's End and Milk Island and channel fish between Gap Head and Straitsmouth," Ms. Lepionka continued. "Also, Woodland Period people had an agricultural settlement near Old Garden Beach and fished off the Headlands. [Stone artifacts from those areas and from the Rockport Country Club and Old Garden Beach grounds are in the collection of the Sandy Bay Historical Society.] All together the evidence points to a native history in your neck of the woods [near my home at the Gap] of at least five thousand years."

The Indians prized horseshoe crabs, which migrated annually to mate on Old Garden beach, for many purposes. They used the tails to tip projectiles, the shells to bail water from canoes and serve as ladles and the bodies as bait for their crab and eel traps. The waters around Straitsmouth and the headlands were a prime fishing area. The Plymouth Colony had a seasonal fishery at Gap Head prior to English settlement of Cape Ann.

Indians were known to inhabit the area just behind Straitsmouth at today's Old Garden Beach near Gully Point. The area was named thus because Indians came down from Maine and New Hampshire each spring to fish, hunt and dig clams. The many caches of stone tools, bones and clams highlight the mobility of Cape Ann's inhabitants in these early days. There were seasonal migrants with campsites and seasonal villages on the Atlantic

Stone weight used to hold fish net underwater; it had a grooved knob around which the netting was wrapped. *Author's collection.*

coastlines. Wamesit was at the junction of the Concord and Merrimack Rivers near Pawtucket Falls, making for a seasonal migration of only thirty miles—a day trip—to Agawam in Ipswich and to Cape Ann.

"They also cleared the area along the beach of trees and bushes and planted corn. Many homeowners have discovered Indian stone hoes and axes and other artifacts including arrow heads in their garden yards," she added. "Sandy Bay Historical Society and Cape Ann Museum has some very fine examples on display. Their method of clearing land was to cut the trees one to three feet from the ground, burn the branches and sow the corn between the stumps, and when the roots became sufficiently pliable, they were taken from the ground. By 1623, when the Dorchester Company arrived to set up fishing stages in Gloucester, there were few traces of savages and little evidence of Indian occupation."

Phillips reported an extensive cache of stone arrowheads along Penzance Road near Land's End in Rockport not far from the old Turks Head Inn and Loblolly Cove.

In 1700, the town meeting deputized Lieutenant William Stevens, an officer in the militia, and Ensign Joseph Allen, a selectman, to make "a full

A seven-inch stone axe blade that was grooved to wrap rawhide to attach the shaft. It appears to be stained with pine tar or another tree resin. *Author's collection.*

compensation about our township with those Indians that hath laid claims to the land of our township."

Samuel English, who claimed to be the grandson of Chief Masconomet, was the leader of the native Indians and demanded payment for the lands now settled by white men and named by them Cape Ann. On February 12, 1702, the town paid the Indians seven pounds for the ten thousand acres of land. The settlers now had clear title to their lands. The final act of incorporation of Gloucester was passed by the General Court in May 1642.

In 1604, Samuel de Champlain came ashore in Whale Cove and met several Pawtucket there. Five or six Indians approached in a canoe after signaling the French barque from Emerson's Point using smoke signals. He went ashore to speak to them and offered each a knife and a biscuit. According to Champlain's journal, the French were not sure where to sail because of all the surprise obstacles around Cape Ann, such as the three Turks Heads islands, so they asked the Indians to draw the coastline to the south. This they did, showing Gloucester Harbor, all the river outlets and all the islands in Boston Bay all the way to Cape Cod. Champlain later returned to Gloucester Harbor in 1606, encountering more than two hundred Indians.

John Babson, in his *History of Gloucester*, stated that "by 1617, three-quarters of the Native American population in Massachusetts had died of common diseases brought from Europe." According to Lepionka, there are divergent opinions about this statement. Native Americans were still in evidence as late as the early 1700s, according to other historical sources.

In Pringle's 1892 book on the *History of the Town and City of Gloucester, Cape Ann*, he stated, "At that time Cape Ann was the home of a thrifty settlement of Red Men." About the Indians living on Cape Ann in 1606, Champlain observed:

> *All the Indians from Island Cape onwards wear no skins or furs.* [Of course, Champlain only saw them wearing summer clothing—Indians naturally wore furs and skins for protection in winter.] *Their clothing was made from grasses and hemp, and barely covered their bodies, coming only down to the thighs. But the men have their privy parts concealed by a small skin. It is the same also with the women, who wear it a little lower behind than the men; all the rest of the body is naked.*
>
> *The men cut off the hair on top of the heads like those at Saco river. I saw, among other things a girl with her hair quite neatly done up by means of a skin dyed red and trimmed on the upper part with little shell beads. Some of her hair hung down behind, while the rest was braided in various ways. These people paint their faces red, black and yellow. They have almost no beard and pull it out as fast as it grows. Their bodies are well proportioned.*
>
> *I do not know what government they have, but believe that in this they resemble their neighbors, who have none. They do not know what it is to worship or pray. They have indeed sundry superstitions, like the other Indians. For weapons they have spears, clubs, bows and arrows. In appearance they seem to be of good disposition, and better than those of the northward: but the whole of them, to tell the truth, are not worth much. The slightest intercourse with them discloses their character. They are great thieves, and if they cannot lay hold of a thing with their hands, try to do so with their feet. I fancy that, had they anything to barter, they would not resort to thievery. They bartered their bows, arrows, and quivers for pins, and buttons, and had they had anything better, would have done the same with it. One must be on one's guard against these people and mistrust them, yet without allowing them to perceive it. They gave us a quantity of tobacco, which they dry and then reduce to powder. When they eat Indian corn, they boil it in earthen pots, which they make in a different way from ours. They crush it also in wooden mortars, and reduce it to flour, and then make cakes and biscuits of it.*

Due to the exposed nature of the section of Cape Ann that is now the town of Rockport, and the evidence that it was densely wooded, it is certain that there were no permanent Indian settlements in this part of the Cape. This is borne out by the extreme sparsity of Indian relics that have been found here. The Indians seen by Champlain at his first Cape Ann landing at Whale Cove, Rockport, were probably living in the vicinity during the summer months to engage in fishing. The Indians of this section belonged to the great Algonquin family. The only local Indian name preserved on the Cape today is Annisquam.

Sagamore, Indian chief of Agawam, now Ipswich, came aboard Governor Winthrop's boat when he came to Sandy Bay in 1630 to fish. There are records of lands on Cape Ann purchased from Indians as late as 1701. Remains of burial grounds have been found in Gloucester and Annisquam and on the islands along the Annisquam River and near Coffin's Beach and Wingaersheek Beach.

Lepionka observed that

> *the sites on the river islands and along the salt marshes were resource procurement sites for digging and processing shellfish. The main village where the people were living was in Riverview just north of Pole Hill. Satellite settlements were behind Wingaersheek* [Old Coffins Farm] *and in Lobster Cove. The people could go to the clam beds and beaches any time they wanted to get shellfish and shells. After the crop harvest, people could choose to stay in the main village, or go visit relatives, or go on trading expeditions or raids, or go to winter camps to hunt bear and moose, or go to set up trap lines to get furs to trade to the Europeans or go ice fishing on lakes at inland winter villages. The people in Essex County had a large winter village in Lowell on the Merrimack, called Wamesit. Extended families operated independently as small bands and had a lot of options. If they moved with the seasons, it was not because they lacked permanent settlements.*

Coastal Algonquin farmed and grew corn, but they also fished, fowled and dug clams, retaining their hunter-gatherer subsistence. The coastal Algonquin were more mobile, less sedentary and more diverse in their practices.

Lepionka stated during our interview:

> *The Coastal Archaic people lived here year-round. They were absorbed or replaced by Eastern Woodland Indians around 3,500 years ago. The Woodland Indians were seasonal migrants up to around a thousand years ago. By then they had become agriculturalists based on the cultivation of maize. They began establishing permanent villages just inland from their*

> *summer camps on the shore. They extended or moved these villages as needed to be near fertile soil for their crops. Corn depletes the soil of nitrogen and must be planted in new ground every two or three years. This is called mobile farming, but it is not the same thing as seasonal migration. The native people here did not over-specialize in agriculture but retained a mixed economy based on fishing, shell fishing, hunting, fowling, gathering and the cultivation of domesticated plants, including corn, squash, pumpkin, beans, peas, sunflower, tobacco, Jerusalem artichoke and amaranth and other chenopodiums* [a genus of numerous species of perennial or annual herbaceous flowering plants].

Speculation about the lack of artifacts was that Indians seldom fished or camped on Straitsmouth Island. As the island is only four hundred feet from the mainland, the Indians could have easily canoed or swum over, but to what purpose? The island is rocky, and fishing from the island shores provide no advantage over fishing from the mainland or from their own canoes. Indians were as busy hunting and fishing as they were farming, growing crops of corn, squash and beans. The dense ledge on the island made it difficult to clear the land to find enough arable soil in which to plant. Also, the fact that it had no freshwater ponds or springs ruled against farming there, whereas streams and brooks proliferated on the mainland. Seals sunning themselves on the eastern end of the island may have brought Indians to the island on day trips to hunt them.

Chapter 2
GEOGRAPHY AND TOPOGRAPHY

STRAITSMOUTH ISLAND

The island consists of more than thirty acres and is located at the eastern end of Gap Head road only about 430 feet from the mainland. The nautical location is 42° 39' 42" North, 70° 35' 12" West. The perimeter measures a little over one mile. Most of the island is made of granite ledge indigenous to Cape Ann. Twenty thousand years ago, Cape Ann was covered by an enormous glacier. As the climate warmed and the ice melted, rocks of all shapes and sizes were left behind. Islands were formed as larger ledges appeared and the waters receded, and the glacier ice slowly melted on its retreat to Greenland. Islands range from single rocks to huge landmasses such as Greenland. There are two main types of island: continental islands and oceanic islands.

Straitsmouth is classified as a continental island, which are found in shallow seas off large landmasses. They were formed when rising seas (for example, at the end of an ice age) cut off part of the land from a continent. Great Britain is another example of a continental island.

Straitsmouth Island was probably part of the mainland and eventually was cut free by ocean storms and violent earthquakes over time. The Gap, which forms a narrow waterway between Gap Head and the island, is only 430 feet across, and at low tide there is a reef that is only under 3 feet of water. This reef runs east to west about halfway through the Gap. This shallow area has been noted on charts as far back as 1776. This waterway was probably called a strait at one time by local fishermen and has formed

Aerial photograph of Straitsmouth Island, taken by a drone in the summer of 2019. *Author's collection.*

the basis of the name Straitsmouth Cove, Landing, Point and Headland, as well as other Straitsmouth appellations over time.

The first people arrived here about eleven thousand years ago. The climate warmed, and tribes migrated to the seashore to fish and grow crops in the summers. Europeans sailed along the Massachusetts coast more than one thousand years ago.

Today, Straitsmouth Island is home to wildlife and many variations of birds. The 1936 issue of *Cape Ann Tourist's Guide*, which sold for twenty-five cents, listed more than two hundred bird species reported by the Rockport Bird Club. Interestingly, when I first stepped foot on the island in 2008, there was not one sea gull to be found. The experts at Mass Audubon were also baffled and surmised that a predator or feral animal was present. The local coyote population has been growing in the area for years. Deer have been seen and photographed, as well as families of wild turkeys on the island. Being only four hundred feet from the mainland, deer can easily swim over. They have been seen on Thacher Island, which is two miles offshore. Seals are frequent visitors at the northern and eastern end and sun themselves at

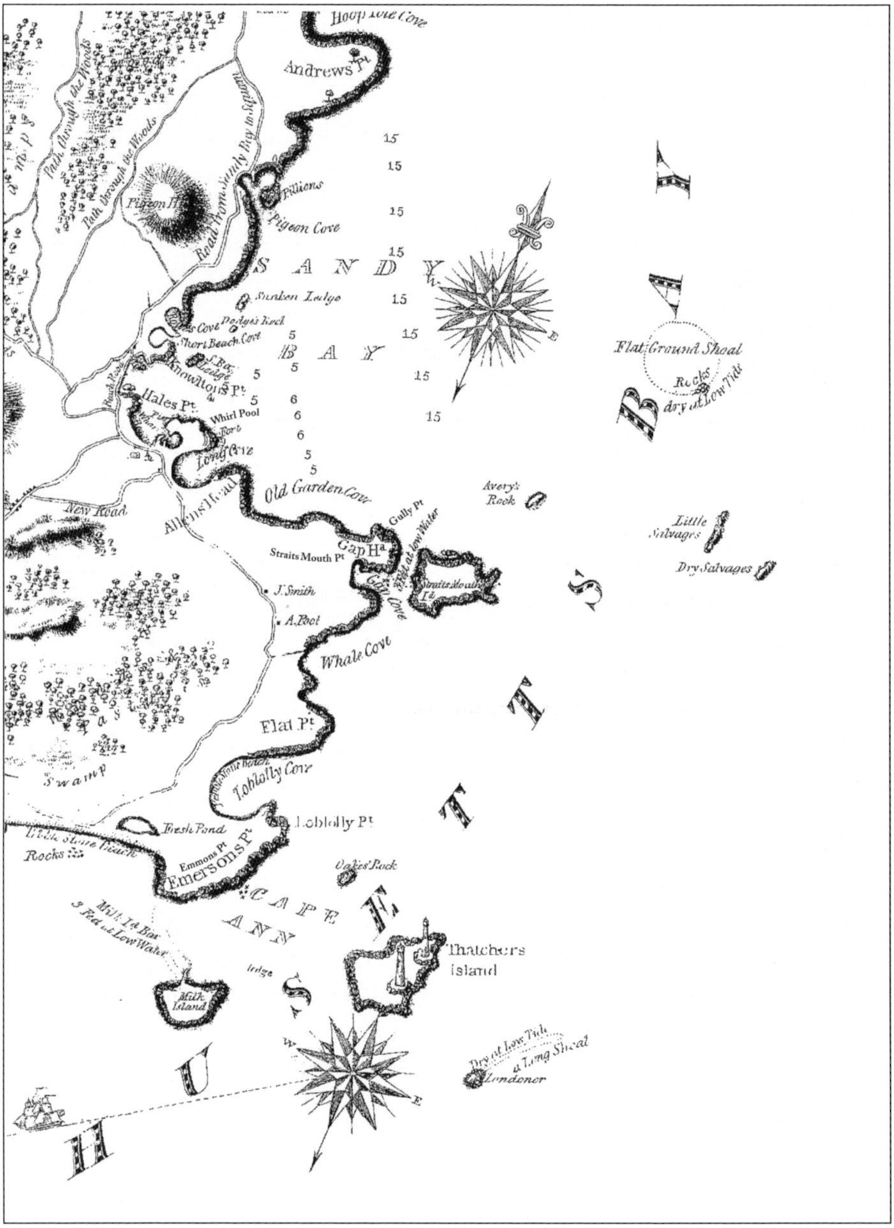

Segment of the 1831 *Map of Gloucester, Cape Ann* by John Mason of the landmarks surrounding Straitsmouth Island, with additional locations added by the author. *Author's collection.*

low tide. We have counted as many as three hundred gray and harbor seals at one time, even in the winter months. Cormorants are often seen drying their wings, an act they perform in a strange posture on the rocky shoreline.

I will confine my discussion of Straitsmouth and the surrounding area to within two or three miles of the island. The jagged coastline from Halibut Point down to Emerson's Point is about sixteen miles long.

Using the segment of the map of the area, seen in this chapter, I will identify the various locations referred to in the book. Starting in the north is Rockport Harbor, which prior to 1811 had been called Long Cove before breakwaters and wharves and Bearskin Neck were built to form a harbor between 1836 and 1840. Just north of Long Cove was an area called the "Whirlpool," which was made up of a small natural cove that funneled water at high tides and seasonal currents, forming a whirlpool. This area was eventually converted to today's Old Harbor as breakwaters and new granite wharves were built. Moving southward, we come to Old Garden Beach (Old Garden Cove); Gully Point; the Gap, which separates Straitsmouth Island from the mainland; Gap Cove (Straitsmouth Cove/Straitsmouth Landing/Straitsmouth Point); Whale Cove; and Loblolly Cove to Emerson's Point (Emmons Point). Thacher Island is across from Whale Cove, and Milk Island is to the southwest of Thacher. Moving farther southwest (not shown on this map) is Salt Island and Good Harbor Beach, and farther south is Braces Cove and Eastern Point at the mouth of Gloucester Harbor.

Many of the explorers, Champlain and Smith particularly, noted the number of islands situated around Cape Ann. When Champlain named the area *Cape Aux Isles* (Cape of Islands), he was impressed with the number of small (as he called them) "unimportant islands" but still was mindful enough to name the area as he did. John Smith went even further when he named the three islands the three Turks Heads, which are today's Straitsmouth, Thacher and Milk Islands.

In addition, there are several reefs and shoals identified on charts. To the northeast of Straitsmouth, for instance, lies Avery's Ledge (Rock); farther to the east the area is known as the Salvages, the Little Salvages (Wet Salvages) and the Dry Salvages, the one that the Thacher family wrecked on in 1635. When Champlain described them in his journaling in 1604, little did he know that Anthony Thacher would fetch up on this same ledge thirty years later in 1635, losing his entire family except for his wife, Elizabeth, and be washed southward to his namesake island, soon to called "Thacher's Woe." The island was given to Thacher by the Massachusetts General Court, sitting at Salem, "toward his greate losses."

THACHER ISLAND

The larger of the three islands is estimated to contain about fifty-four acres, most of which consists of good soil, affording rich pasturage for a few cattle. In 1714, it was purchased by Reverend John White from Anthony Thacher for £100. He sold it for £275 in 1727 to Joseph Allen of Gloucester, who used it to graze his oxen. In 1771, the Allen heirs sold it to three Gloucester men (John Low, Samuel Plummer and William Ellery), who in turn sold it to a committee of six men (John Hancock, Captain Nathaniel Allen, Major Richard Reed, Captain Richard Derby, John Erving and Captain John Patrick Tracy). They had been authorized by the Massachusetts Bay Colony to buy the island to "erect a lighthouse or houses, and a convenient house for the keeper." The colonial government now became its owner, at a cost of £500, and proceeded in the same year to erect two forty-foot-tall lighthouses and a dwelling house on it. The lights were lit for the first time, December 21, 1771. At the commencement of the Revolutionary War, the keeper of the lights, James Kirkwood, was forcibly removed from the island by Captain Rogers's company of Gloucester minutemen because Kirkwood was thought to be a Tory. The lights were extinguished and not relighted until 1784, and eventually they were taken over by the new federal government in 1790. The first keeper, Samuel Huston, was appointed by Secretary of the Treasury Alexander Hamilton. The current 125-foot-tall granite towers were built in 1861 at the outbreak of the Civil War.

THE LONDONER

Situated to the east of Thacher Island, this was a major "dangerous spot in the ocean" named after the ship *London*, which fetched up on those rocks in the early 1600s. It was originally called Gannet Rock and, before that, Fisher Rock. Captain Josiah Sturgis, aboard the U.S. Revenue Cutter Service schooner *Hamilton*, surveyed the reef on June 28, 1845. His chart showed the reef to be ninety feet long and fifty-seven feet wide. Sixty-five shipwrecks had been reported on the Londoner since 1775. Today, the reef is still marked by a tall iron spindle measuring four feet in diameter and forty feet in height, which was erected in 1855. It was originally "surmounted by an octagonal lattice or open-work cast iron day-mark, seven feet high and five feet in diameter," which is no longer there. The spindle still stands five hundred yards offshore about midway between the two lighthouse towers.

OAKES ROCK

In the waters of Loblolly Cove, there is a huge submerged rock called Oakes Rock that is marked by navigation buoys to warn mariners of this unseen danger that even today, as vessels pass through at low tide, can mangle one's outboard motor. The area waters between Thacher and Loblolly Cove are about seventy-three feet deep but only about five feet deep where Oakes Rock lies and around the red nun buoy. Originally named Crackwood's Rock, it was described by Lemuel Gott in his *History of Rockport* as "about a gun shot from the western part of Thacher's." Some have erroneously thought that this was the rock that Reverend John Avery and the Thacher family had struck in 1635. More recent research has proven that more than likely their pinnace had fetched up on the Dry Salvages and the wreckage was blown down wind toward Thacher Island's western shore. We are not sure how it got the name Oakes Rock, although there were a few Oakes families living in the area in the early 1700s, one of whom could have wrecked on the rock.

Not long after the Battle of Bunker Hill an English brig was discovered anchored in the fog near the rock. Captain John Rowe, who had fought at Bunker Hill, rowed out to capture it. It was carrying a cargo of cattle, arms and provisions for the British troops in Boston. The cargo was salvaged and sent to George Washington's troops in Dorchester.

The tramp steamer *City of Lahore*, out of Liverpool, from India to Boston, ran aground in rain and thick fog on Oakes Rock at about 10:00 a.m. on August 22, 1917. It got off without assistance at about 11:30 a.m. The fog signal was heard for about fifteen minutes before the steamer struck.

MILK ISLAND

Lying a short distance south of Thacher's, this island rises but little above the level of the sea. Its soil is enough for the pasturage of a few sheep or cows. It is about fourteen acres, and from 1840 to 1860, sheep were kept there. Originally, it was known as Snake Island because of a long sand spit emanating from Emerson's Point in a curving manner simulating the form of a snake, with the island as its head. Over time, farmers looking for summer grazing land drove their cattle down from Cogswell Farm Landing across the spit and onto this lush island with its own freshwater pond. The first settlers to have cows there were Peter Bennett, who lived on Witham's Beach (Pebble Beach), and Peter Emmons at Loblolly in 1708. In 1718, the island was sold by Bennett along with his house to his brother Anthony, of Gloucester, for forty-seven pounds. Peter Bennett then moved to Georgetown, Maine. At various times, fishing stations existed. Peter Bennett was also a wood loader living near Pebble Beach. On Milk Island, because of the pond, marshland duck blinds had once existed into the twentieth century.

In 1792, Daniel Young and Isaac Jacobs drowned on the treacherous Milk Island bar while bound from Sandy Bay to Salem. The island was also the scene of the fatal wreck of the *Renown* on December 15, 1797.

On Friday, January 23, 1857, the brig *Waverly* went ashore on Milk Island in weather eighteen degrees below zero. A crew of Rockporters got a lifeboat to the stranded vessel and rescued the frostbitten sailors. Much of *Waverly*'s cargo of coffee was saved in a damaged condition, and the brig was later refloated. The day after, Rockport Harbor was frozen from Pigeon Cove to Straitsmouth "as to appear as if one sheet, the ice cakes, all touching together….It was never before so seen," as noted in Marshall Swan's book *Town on Sandy Bay*. John Parsons and Charles Hodgkins bought Milk Island in May 1881 to run "a brisk fish business" there.

In September 1901, Roger Babson, an enterprising entrepreneur, acquired Milk Island. He unveiled his scheme in an open letter: "You may be interested to know that I am corresponding with Sig. Marconi relative to a Wireless Telegraphy Station on Milk Island. If Sig. Marconi makes Newfoundland his American terminus, he may desire to repeat his messages from Newfoundland to Milk Island, and use said plant as a distributing center." Marconi preferred Cape Cod for his eventual station, and the Babsons finally decided that Milk Island was better for birds.

The island was presented to the Commonwealth of Massachusetts by Grace Knight Babson. Today, it is owned by the State of Massachusetts and administered by the state Department of Fish and Game, Marine Fisheries Division, and continues as a bird sanctuary. No one lives on the island.

Emerson's Point (Emmons Point)

In 1708, a man named Peter Emmons had a house opposite Milk Island. The point had been called Emmons Point on early charts and has been erroneously referred to as Emerson Point since the 1800s after Emmons moved away. It was from this point that Indians signaled Champlain traveling from Whale Cove to Gloucester Harbor in 1605. A lifesaving station was built there in 1886, managed by volunteers of the Massachusetts Humane Society.

WHALE COVE

In March 1798, a seventy-six-foot whale was driven ashore, thus providing the name for the area since that time; it was once known as Steep Bank Cove. The whale provided forty barrels of sperm oil. Because it was winter, barrels had to be carried to the top of the bank by sleighs. Descendants of Andrew Lane III related that the leftover blubber was deposited on one of his fields, which has since been known as "The Blubber Lot." The infusion of the blubber as fertilizer increased the production of hay crops from two crops per year to three. This cove had its share of shipwrecks. In 1830, a sloop from Nantucket ran aground, trapping a woman inside for hours until she could be sawed free.

LOBLOLLY COVE

An often-asked question locally, besides "Why are there two lighthouses on Thacher Island?" is "What is Loblolly?" Originally, according to a dictionary, loblolly meant a thick oatmeal gruel; another definition was that it was a kind of tree that grows down south but not in this area.

A magazine article in 1939 recounted that Frank Haskell, who ran an outdoor shore dinner restaurant called Haskell's Camp at Loblolly Cove in the 1920s, had a guest who was a Welshman who said after his meal at Frank's restaurant "that it was a wonderful loblolly." He went on to say that when he was a boy back in Wales, the best part of the lobster was the loblolly, the liver or fat of the lobster, that greenish material you see after you have boiled the crustacean. He used to spread it on bread because they never had much butter.

Frank went on to do some research and learned that Loblolly Cove was named and owned Peter Emmons, also a Welshman, who received a grant of ten acres from the Commonwealth of Massachusetts in about 1700 and named it Loblolly Cove. After learning from his Welsh guest about loblolly, he put two and two together and figured that the original Welshman Emmons had indeed named the area because of the predominance of lobsters to be found along the shore in the 1700s. In those days, it was recorded that lobsters were so plentiful that they could easily be caught in the seaweed and popples at low tide without a trap.

Loblolly was sometimes called Lighthouse Landing because of its proximity to Thacher, and it was identified on some charts as a U.S. government landing for materials going to Thacher. It was also the location where the lighthouse keepers would drop their children off for school having rowed them the one mile from Thacher. They would proceed the two miles to the one-room schoolhouse on Mount Pleasant Street near downtown Rockport, now the restored Boy Scout Hall. Haskell's Camp was also noted for hosting shore dinners for President William Howard Taft and his entourage in 1910.

SALT ISLAND

This small five-acre island stands about one thousand yards from Good Harbor Beach at Brier Neck. A sandbar links the island with the beach at low tide. A distressing shipwreck occurred in 1796. Early in January, the ship *Industry*, with Captain Miles Barnes, belonging to Boston, was lost on Little Good Harbor Beach, near Salt Island, in a violent snowstorm. The logbook, which was kept until eight o'clock, indicated that it had sailed from Portsmouth, England, on November 3 in ballast—meaning it had no cargo and only ballast stone in its hold to keep the big transport deep into the water. All hands perished. The bodies were found and buried from the First Parish Church. The owner of the ship bore public testimony to "the attention and humanity of our citizens on this melancholy occasion." In the nineteenth century, the original owner, John Parsons, operated a lobstering business there.

In 1919, parts of the Fox Film Corporation movie *Bride Number 13* were shot on location at Good Harbor Beach and Salt Island. This was to be an epic pirate adventure. A castle was built on Salt Island. This was later to be blown up as the heroes made their escape. A shipwreck scene was staged at Brace Cove where a vessel was set afire and blown up. The half-sunken old schooner, *Mineola*, laid up at the Davis Dock in Gloucester Harbor, was chosen to play the wreck. It was refloated and rigged to resemble a

Salt Island was a movie location in 1919 that required a castle to be built. *CAM.*

pirate ship with yardarms, a crow's nest and square rigged. Two of the principal actors had fallen into the sea and had to be rescued from the frigid November water and taken to Addison Gilbert Hospital suffering from exposure. Later that day, the schooner was rigged with explosives and incendiaries and the deck doused with oil. The old schooner was blown up and erupted into flames, burning to the waterline within minutes. The 1860 vessel went out with a bang.

The fifteen-part serial silent film was at the time "the costliest picture ever made...would consume expenditures of at least one million dollars." It was conceived and written by Edward Sedgwick, directed by Richard Stanton (aka "Salt Island's Mighty Emperor") and starred Marguerite Clayton, Jack O'Brien and Ed Rossman. The script was inspired by "Ali Baba and the Forty Thieves." "This island was an island at high tide and part of the mainland at low tide. Fox film Co. was building a wooden castle on the island, which was about one hundred feet high and hosted the actions of this silent film," read a story in the local press.

In the 1940s, Guy Parsons used one of the old family fishing shacks as a summer place. In 1952, the Parsons family sold Salt Island. In 1959, James Kimball purchased Salt Island for $2,000. Salt Island was listed for sale at $300,000 plus beach parking passes for the family in 2013. Most recently in 2017, Salt Island was again listed for sale, at $750,000. Conservationists and environmentalists were hoping to buy the island.

THE BREAKWATER

This breakwater was started in 1885 by the federal government to form a "Harbor of Refuge" and a deep-water port for U.S. naval vessels and other vessels traveling the waters along the Massachusetts coast. The plans called for a long breakwater one and a half miles long that stretched from Avery's Ledge to Abner's Ledge and then dog-legged northwest toward Andrews Point. It would be large enough to hold five thousand ships and was planned to hold the entire North Atlantic Fleet of the U.S. Navy and cover an area of 1,664 acres. The project was abandoned in 1915 with only nine hundred feet completed. Today, only three hundred feet remain as storms, and hurricanes have knocked down many of the remaining twenty-five-ton granite blocks. Ironically, this Harbor of Refuge was to be built to provide safe harbor for vessels proceeding along the coast, but it has now become a dangerous marine hazard.

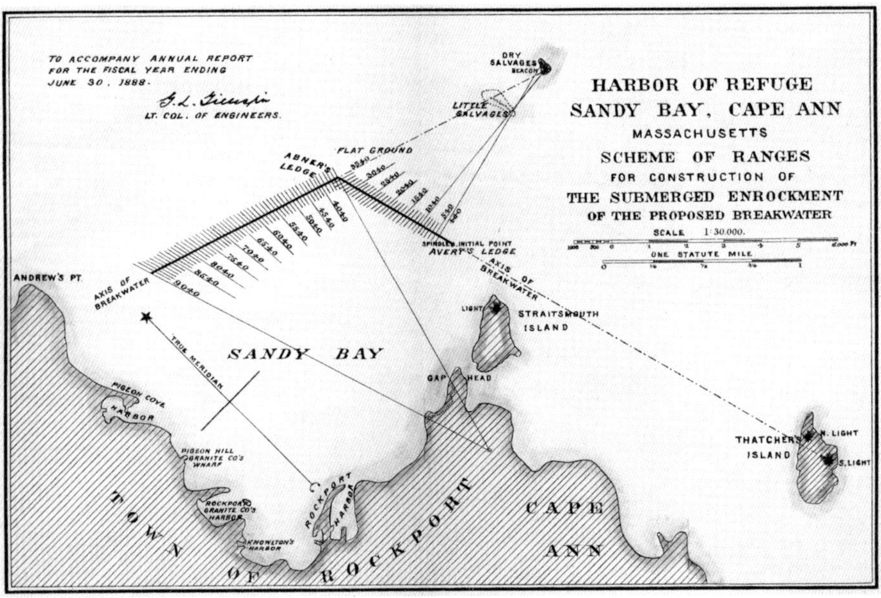

A chart of the proposed Harbor of Refuge breakwater that would encompass 1,664 acres and provide protection for more than five thousand ships. *SBHS.*

AVERY'S LEDGE (ROCK)

This ledge is located at the southern terminus of the government breakwater just north of Straitsmouth and is marked by a bell buoy. It was named by Anthony Thacher in his letter to his brother as "Avery his Fall" to commemorate his cousin Reverend John Avery, lost with his entire family in the hurricane of 1635. Later researchers and historians have concluded that this was not the ledge he was wrecked on. John Greenleaf Whittier (1807–1892) once commemorated Avery's death in his poem "Swan Song of Parson Avery" in 1858:

When the reaper's task was ended, and the summer wearing late,
Parson Avery sailed from Newbury, with his wife and children eight,
Dropping down the river-harbor in the shallop "Watch and Wait."

Pleasantly lay the clearings in the mellow summer-morn,
With the newly planted orchards dropping their fruits first born,
And the home-roofs like brown islands amid a sea of corn.

Broad meadows reached out seaward the tided creeks between,
And hills rolled wave-like inland, with oaks and walnuts green:
A fairer home, a goodlier land, his eyes had never seen.

Yet away sailed Parson Avery, away where duty led,
And the voice of God seemed calling, to break the living bread
To the souls of fishers starving on the rocks of Marblehead.

All day they sailed: at nightfall the pleasant land-breeze died,
The blackening sky, at midnight, its starry lights denied,
And far and low the thunder of tempest prophesied!

Blotted out were all the coastlines, gone were rock, and wood, and sand;
Grimly anxious stood the skipper with the rudder in his hand,
And questioned of the darkness what sea was and what was land.

And the preacher heard his dear ones, nestled round him, weeping sore:
"Never heed, my little children! Christ is walking on before
To the pleasant land of heaven, where the sea shall be no more."

All at once the great cloud parted, like a curtain drawn aside,
To let down the torch of lightning on the terror far and wide;
And the thunder and the whirlwind together smote the tide.

There was wailing in the shallop, woman's wail and man's despair,
A crash of breaking timbers on the rocks so sharp and bare,
And, through it all, the murmur of Father Avery's prayer.

From his struggle in the darkness with the wild waves and the blast,
On a rock, where every billow broke above him as it passed,
Alone, of all his household, the man of God was cast.

There a comrade heard him praying, in the pause of wave and wind:
"All my own have gone before me, and I linger just behind;
Not for life I ask, but only for the rest Thy ransomed find!

"In this night of death, I challenge the promise of Thy word!—
Let me see the great salvation of which mine ears have heard!—
Let me pass from hence forgiven, through the grace of Christ, our Lord!

"In the baptism of these waters wash white my every sin,
And let me follow up to Thee my household and my kin!
Open the sea-gate of Thy heaven and let me enter in!"

When the Christian sings his death-song, all the listening heavens draw near,
And the angels, leaning over the walls of crystal, hear
How the notes so faint and broken swell to music in God's ear.

The ear of God was open to His servant's last request;
As the strong wave swept him downward the sweet hymn upward pressed,
And the soul of Father Avery went, singing, to its rest.

There was wailing on the mainland, from the rocks of Marblehead;
In the stricken church of Newbury, the notes of prayer were read;
And long, by board and hearthstone, the living mourned the dead.

And still the fishers outbound, or scudding from the squall,
With grave and reverent faces, the ancient tale recall,
When they see the white waves breaking on the Rock of Avery's Fall!

ABNER'S LEDGE

This ledge marks the outer point of the government breakwater built between 1880 and 1919. It was at this point that the breakwater took a dogleg to the west toward Andrews Point.

HALIBUT POINT ("HAUL-ABOUT-POINT")

The origin of the name Halibut Point is not wholly clear, but the most commonly accepted explanation is that early settlers in sailing around the Cape to or from Ipswich Bay had to "haul about" their boats and reset their sails when they rounded that point. There are also a few allusions in local documents to "holybut point." Presently, the words, as in so many other place names, have become corrupted into "Halibut Point."

GULLY POINT

Sometimes referred to as Gully Cove, this is off Marmion Way near Gap Head Road. It was here, reportedly, where Caleb Norwood found pirates gold in 1770. More on this story can be found in the sixth chapter on privateers and pirates.

SALVAGES

The ocean side of the outer breakwater is a mean area of rocks, ledges and shallow water known as the flat ground and the Salvages. The Salvages consist of two rock formations, Dry Salvages (the last syllable rhymes with "wages"), about a mile east of the breakwater, and Little Salvages, five hundred yards closer to the breakwater. The meaning is unclear except that part of the rock outcrop is above the tide line and therefore dry, while another part (Little Salvages) is submerged at high tide. Captain John Smith wrote "salvages" for "savages," from the French *sauvage*. The maritime historian Samuel Eliot

Morrison pointed out that they have always been a menace to navigators around Cape Ann. Colonial records for the late 1600s refer to dry salvages as "a rock called salvages." Lambert's 1812 *New Chart of Massachusetts Bay* shows "salvages" along with a scattering of dots to represent the two salvages and the flat ground. It is speculated that the local fishermen equated the treacherous red men ("savages") with the dangerous ledges, hence the name given to the reefs. Dry Salvages are above water in fair weather and visible from the mainland and from out to sea, but because of poor visibility, many ships have been lost there. Many of the old tombstones, the records of those captured or killed by Indians, read in the quaint language of the day, "Captivated by Salvages." Locally today, the word is accented on the second syllable ("sal-*vag*-es").

John Babson reported that in 1768, a vessel sailing from Nova Scotia to Boston ran into it. The sea was so rough that a boat of residents could not get aboard. The next day, four bodies lay on the rocks. The other sixteen passengers and crew were not found. Since the early period, vessels have continued to run aground on the Salvages. In 1961, it was a Liberty ship and in 1953 a converted subchaser, with other boats following in more recent years. In September 1963, the navy minesweeper USS *Grouse* ran

The Salvages is the home for hundreds of gray and harbor seals who sun themselves at low tide. *Author's collection.*

aground on Little Salvages. All thirty crew members were saved, but after many attempts to move it off the reefs had failed, the navy doused the 136-foot wooden vessel with gasoline and burned it to the waterline. For many years, a 30-foot-high red tripod stood to alert mariners to the danger, but it was removed in 1945. Today, a bellboy marks it half a mile to the northeast.

The origin of the name is not clear. Champlain's only comment on the Salvages was "another low island upon which the sea brakes." Morrison favored the origin of the name to be a transfer from a rock known as the Savage Rock off the coast of New Hampshire seen by Gosnold in 1602. Rockport's historian Ebenezer Pool, who had also examined this evidence, disagreed with this reasoning, which had been advanced in Pool's day. A more likely explanation may be that expressed by Peter Gott in the mid-1850s in the *Cape Ann Fisherman* that the name comes from the appearance of "savages" (Indians). Other theories included the fact that so many vessels have wrecked there that maritime salvage operations were conducted there frequently. Whatever the origin of the name, T.S. Eliot's "The Dry Salvages," the third poem of his *Four Quartets of 1941*, has brought additional fame to Rockport. Here follows an excerpt:

The river is within us, the sea is all about us;
The sea is the land's edge also, the granite
Into which it reaches, the beaches where it tosses
Its hints of earlier and other creation:
The starfish, the hermit crab, the whale's backbone;
The pools where it offers to our curiosity
The more delicate algae and the sea anemone.
It tosses up our losses, the torn seine,
The shattered lobsterpot, the broken oar
And the gear of foreign dead men.
The sea has many voices,
Many gods and many voices.
The salt is on the briar rose,
The fog is in the fir trees.
The sea howl
And the sea yelp, are different voices
Often together heard; the whine in the rigging,
The menace and caress of wave that breaks on water,
The distant rote in the granite teeth,
And the wailing warning from the approaching headland

Are all sea voices, and the heaving groaner
Rounded homewards, and the seagull:
And under the oppression of the silent fog
The tolling bell
Measures time not our time, rung by the unhurried
Ground swell, a time
Older than the time of chronometers, older
Than time counted by anxious worried women
Lying awake, calculating the future,
Trying to unweave, unwind, unravel
And piece together the past and the future,
Between midnight and dawn, when the past is all deception,
The future futureless, before the morning watch
When time stops and time is never ending;
And the ground swell, that is and was from the beginning,
Clangs the bell.
Aground on the Dry Salvages.

Eliot, who spent summers on Eastern Point in Gloucester, knew the Salvages from having sailed past it many times as a resident.

FLAT GROUND SHOAL

This ledge is located just to the north of the Little Salvages to the east of the Harbor of Refuge Breakwater and between the flashing green gong and the green bell buoy. In fact, it is a series of three ledges; the northernmost has ten feet, the middle one thirteen and the southernmost rock only two feet and is bare at spring low tides. Charts warn mariners to stay north to the green bell buoy, as it runs for about half a nautical mile and varies in depth from three to fifteen feet. The waters around Sandy Bay generally run from thirty-five to eighty-five feet deep. The Liberty ship *Charles S. Haight* was sunk here in 1946, and its engine block is seen at very low tides near the red nun "2" buoy northeast of the breakwater. Its binnacle now resides at the Sandy Bay Yacht Club in Rockport Harbor.

KEEPING THE STRAITSMOUTHS STRAIGHT

It is sometimes difficult to keep the various Straitsmouth name locations straight, starting with Straitsmouth Cove, otherwise known today as Gap Cove. Before Sandy Bay was settled, this cove was a fishing center and shipping point for lumber and other goods. The fishermen who came from Essex and Ipswich had fishing stands that they operated for only part of the year. After soaking their catch in brine and sun-drying it, they shipped it to the Caribbean and to other European destinations in wooden barrels made at the cooperage on Beaver Dam in Pigeon Cove. The cove had no wharves. Vessels were run aground and then loaded.

These early fishermen were bold sailors. They were among the first to venture from Cape Ann to the grounds off Cape Sable in Nova Scotia. The first permanent settlement of the cove was by John Babson, who in 1695 received a grant of two or three acres "at the strait mouth point to set up fishing upon." Fishing apparently was not to his liking, because within a few years, he had sold the property to Joshua Norwood, after whom the cove was called for a while. At one time, there may have been three houses around the cove, but toward the end of the century, no one lived there. Ebenezer Pool's reference to a possible settlement in the cove by fishermen from Plymouth between 1625 and 1630 has not been verified by historians. According to Pool, Governor Winslow, of the Plymouth colony, had a house frame and material brought from England to Plymouth and then to Straitsmouth for "[f]owling, fishing, lumbering and trading with the Indians."

In the early 1800s, the Massachusetts Humane Society established a lifesaving station on the cove manned by volunteers. Years later, the U.S. Coast Guard station replaced it. After World War II, it was discontinued, and the property and the beach sold to private owners.

The first reference found regarding Straitsmouth Landing was by Ebenezer Pool, who called it Straitsmouth Rock Landing, but no location was given. At first, it seemed that this was another name for Straitsmouth Cove Landing, but a later reference to a Straitsmouth Head Landing appeared in a list of landings between Old Garden Landing and the Cove landing, which suggested that it was a separate landing. This was confirmed by an 1800 document in the City of Gloucester archives. It had today's Straitsmouth Way, called the "Main Road," leading to three landings. The first was Straitsmouth Cove. The second was Straitsmouth Rock Landing, which was reached by following the "Cart Road" (Gap Head Road) northeast from the end of the Main Road and then east onto Straitsmouth Head. The third landing was Old Garden, northwest from the cart road. The exact location of Straitsmouth Rock Landing was not given, but it appeared that it must be somewhere on today's Gap Head.

Seafarers in the 1600s did not restrict their landings to beaches and coves. This forgotten landing would likely consist of a rock or ledge face vertical to the ocean, allowing space for a vessel to tie up and water deep enough for loading at low and high tide. On my personal explorations on private property at Gap Head, I came across an area that slopes down from Gap Head Road through private property that would have allowed easy access for cargo. The landing was probably discovered and used by fishermen and woodcutters who in the 1600s operated out of Straitsmouth Cove, shipping timber and dry fish. It was probably used until permanent wharves were built in the Old Harbor and Long Cove in the early 1830s. The entire area behind Straitsmouth Island along Marmion Way at the Gap was called the Straitsmouth District or Straitsmouth Point, which included a large area in which some of the first settlers first built small log cabins.

THE NEIGHBORS: STRAITSMOUTH LIFE-SAVING STATION AND THE STRAITSMOUTH INN

Straitsmouth Point area shared two other structures that were important historically. One was the lifesaving station at Gap Cove, which was built in 1887 to replace Davis Point Life-Saving Station in Annisquam, which closed because the new location in the Gap was closer to where many wrecks seemed to be occurring and was in an area less exposed to frequent northeast storms. On July 1, 1902, it was renamed Straitsmouth Life-Saving Station and had eight surfmen stationed there, including Captain Charles A. Bearse in 1903. According to the U.S. Coast Guard, the first keeper of the station (Davis Point Station) was Jabez Marchant Jr., who was appointed in 1874 at the age of thirty-five and who resigned on January 4, 1896. Next was Charles A. Bearse, appointed on February 3, 1896, and assigned to Gap Cove in 1900. Next came Frank E. Aubin, who was acting keeper for a time until his appointment on November 12, 1915; Robert F. Pierce, who was reassigned from the Orleans station on July 6, 1921, and who retired on December 11, 1923; and John J. Glynn, who was keeper from October 15, 1927, until June

20, 1932. Glynn was followed by Chief Boatswains Mate S.H. Cobbett, but Glynn returned on July 20, 1934, and remained until July 18, 1935. He was followed by Everett M. Mills, who arrived on July 12, 1935, and remained until November 4, 1937.

The federal government had established the U.S. Life-Saving Service in 1872, eventually building 280 stations. On Cape Ann in the Massachusetts District, there were 15 stations, each sequentially numbered as Plum Island, designated No. 1; Davis Neck, No. 2; and Gap Cove, No. 3. Others were located in Rockport on Middle Street on Bearskin Neck, No. 4, and at Emerson's Point, No. 5. In 1869, the Massachusetts Humane Society (a sister organization dedicated to lifesaving) established what was called a "hut of refuge" on Milk Island, operated by William Stillman. These huts were small sheds supplied with clothing, food and essentials for shipwrecked mariners and were placed along the Massachusetts shoreline, eventually numbering 92.

The Straitsmouth Life-Saving Station at Gap Cove was where the members of the U.S. Coast Guard living on Straitsmouth were sent in 1937 when the keeper house was closed and the island eventually sold. The new USCG station at Gap Cove (still called Straitsmouth Station) remained open and staffed until it was closed in 1964. During World War II, it was an important submarine watch station. A large 156-foot-high radio tower and antenna was constructed and used as a viewing platform looking for enemy ships and submarines. The aerial photo shows the number "22" on the lawn of the station, indicating that it was USCG Station 22 from the air. In 1968, it was sold to a private individual who coincidentally was a marine admiralty attorney.

The Straitsmouth Inn was on Gap Head road leading toward Gap Head itself. It was built and operated by Mrs. Everett (Ella) R. Wilkinson and opened on June 22, 1907. It was a large structure that regularly accommodated more than one hundred guests. It employed many young women as housemaids and waitresses who lived just down the road in the inn's employee boardinghouse at the corner of Straitsmouth Way and Marmion Way. This inn was a favorite of tourists from Boston and New York, who came annually by train and were picked up in a stagecoach at the Rockport train station. It had a tennis court just below the inn on a ledge overlooking Straitsmouth Island and a boathouse and boat ramp just across the Gap.

During the late 1890s, the hotel industry was booming on Cape Ann, as were new residential properties and subdivisions in Rockport. Stonehaven

The Straitsmouth Life-Saving Station no. 22 at Gap Head adjacent to Straitsmouth Island. *SBHS.*

The Straitsmouth Inn on Gap Head Road could accommodate one hundred guests. *SBHS.*

was the name given to the area bounded by Marmion Way, from South Street around to Shetland Road and Gap Head Road and completed by Straitsmouth Way. A real estate ad in the local press read, "Over 70 beautiful lots have already been laid out. The hotel has been situated on Gap Head. The whole estate comprises about 70 acres, every inch of which is eligible for seaside cottage lots." The Rockport Board of Trade published a newspaper in July 1901, *The Review*, which promoted the area with a regular column called "Marmion Way Notes," with trivia of transparent interest such as news of tennis courts marked out in response to the reawakened popularity of that pastime, the lures of the public lifesavers drill held Mondays and Thursday mornings at ten o'clock at the U.S. Life-Saving Station and reports of the newly opened Straitsmouth Inn. It burned down on New Year's Eve, December 31, 1960. Ten years later, the Turks Head Inn at the south end near Loblolly Cove burned to the ground, two of the many grand inns and hotels that succumbed to fire over the years.

NAVAL AIR DISASTER ON MARMION WAY

On July 12, 1954, a young twenty-four-year-old navy pilot, Ensign John J. Schlock, flying from Quonset Point Naval Air Station, Rhode Island, was killed when he crashed his flaming Douglas Skyraider (attack bomber) into the woods on Marmion Way before the eyes of his horrified fiancée, who was employed at the Seaward Inn on Marmion Way adjacent to Gap Cove (Straitsmouth Cove). He was killed instantly, and the wreckage was strewn over a wide area next to the estate of Albert K. Huckins at 110 Marmion Way. Huckins was sitting in his living room at the time and was uninjured. The back end of the engine landed within fifty feet of his house, while the main section of the plane plowed through the woods, coming to rest two thousand yards away, behind the house of Dr. C. Frederick Sprague at 112 Marmion Way. I myself now live in Sprague's former house on Marmion Way and next door to the old Huckins estate.

The crash was witnessed by two waitresses from the Straitsmouth Inn who were sunbathing on the grounds of the Straitsmouth Coast Guard station nearby. They described two planes flying in formation buzzing the Coast Guard station radio tower at least four times before one rose and did a loop over the area, clipping the treetops on its descent and then bursting

Douglas A-1 Skyraider attack bomber, like the one that crashed off Marmion Way in 1954. *From Pixdaus.com.*

into flames. Coast Guardsmen from the Straitsmouth station responded immediately to aid the Rockport fire and police departments. The Coast Guard jeep was the first on the scene. Fear that live ammunition from the wrecked plane might explode from the heat and perhaps kill onlookers caused the police to clear the area. Ensign Schlock's fiancée, Miss Mary Alice Smith, twenty-one years old, a summertime waitress at the Seaward Inn, was treated for shock. The other plane was flown by Schlock's best friend and roommate, Ensign David Johnson, who came to Rockport the next day to visit Miss Smith. Not all tragedies near Straitsmouth Island are of the marine variety.

Chapter 3

EXPLORERS, 1245–1650

This chapter will tell the story of the third Turks Head, Straitsmouth Island. I will confine my discussion to the area then known (1600s) as Sandy Bay Parish, a section of Gloucester in the northeast corner of Cape Ann. Today, it is the town of Rockport, having separated from Gloucester in 1840. In addition, I will focus in the area closest to Straitsmouth Island around the Gap Head, Marmion Way and the Gully Point neighborhood, originally called Straitsmouth Point or the Straitsmouth District in charts and maps of the 1700 and 1800s.

Rockport has a population of about 7,500 in its six and a half square miles. Bordered on the north and east by the Atlantic Ocean, to the south and west lies Gloucester, the city with which Rockport shares Cape Ann. It juts out into the Atlantic and is the first land seen by vessels heading to Boston.

In the early 1400s, before any French or English explorers had set foot in New England, Rockport was but a large chunk of granite. Forest and dense scrub occupied the few areas where sandy soil had been deposited by retreating glaciers. Because of the harshness of the land, the native population was restricted to a few summer visitors who came to hunt, fish and conduct shell fishing.

Straitsmouth Island is separated from it by a narrow channel only a few hundred feet in width. Its surface is rocky and covers about thirty acres.

JOHN SMITH

In 1614, John Smith (1580–1631) anchored in what would later be called Sandy Bay. Casting his eyes over the landscape, he saw the homes of the Agawam Indians in the distance. Along the coast, he saw a "fair headland… fronted by three isles." The three islands he saw near the cape he dubbed the Turks Heads, in memory of his triumph over three Turkish gladiators during his imprisonment.

Smith made this one voyage to the coast of Massachusetts and Maine in 1614. He was both a president and a prisoner in the Jamestown colony of Virginia. Smith was a veteran soldier, sailor, traveler, explorer, mercenary, cartographer and colonist. He was seeking a new area for trade and colonial opportunities for King Charles I. He saw a prosperous fishery to the north, where cod were taken by ships from Portugal, Holland and Spain. Fur trapping and fur trading were practiced by the French and Dutch. He saw New England as a place where the English could settle and prosper. Smith identified three staples that would become the mainstay of the people: timber, fish and stone. His foresight led to the use of just about all the trees around Cape Ann to build ships, docks, wharves and ships masts. Wood became scarce, so much so that the colony had to put a restriction on the amount residents could harvest to twenty cords per year specifically for their fireplaces. So much timber was going to other nations and cities that the local woodlots were being depleted. Fishing has been the major industry since 1623, and granite quarrying was king from 1820 until 1935. Smith went so far as to publish a sixty-page tract of his adventures, which he gave to the king and distributed around England. His *Description of*

Captain John Smith named the Three Turks Heads on his voyage in 1614, now named Straitsmouth, Thacher and Milk Islands. *Author's collection.*

New England, published in 1616, describes the fishing, soils, inhabitants, fauna, flora and climate of the coastal region from Cape Cod to Penobscot in Maine.

I have transcribed a segment directly from Smith's book that captures his written words that preserves the spelling and punctuation of the original. Note that the letter *u* is a *v* in most words. I have noted the current name next to each Indian name and location taken from his map of New England he created in 1624 and other references. This short segment centers on his discovering the three Turks Heads islands. He seems very impressed with the area and calls the "Countrie of the Massachusetts, which is the Paradise of all those parts":

> *Naimkeck* [Salem], *though it be more rockie ground (for Angoam* [could be Sandy Bay or Ipswich or Plumb Island] *is sandie) not much inferior; neither for the harbor, nor anything I could perceiue, but the multitude of people. From hence doth stretch into the Sea the faire headland Tragabigzanda* [Cape Anne], *fronted with three Iles called the three Turks heads* [Straitsmouth, Thacher, Milk Islands today]*: to the North of this, doth enter a great Bay* [probably Ipswich Bay], *where wee founde some habitations and corne fields: they report a great Riuer* [Merrimac River], *and at least thirtie habitations, doo possesse this Countrie. But because the French had got their Trade, I had no leasure to discouer it. The Iles of Mattahunts* [two islands in Ipswich Bay with groves, gardens and corn fields] *are on the West side of this Bay, where are many Iles, and questionlesse good harbors: and then the Countrie of the Massachusets, which is the Paradise of all those parts: for, here are many Iles all planted with corne; groues, mulberries, saluage* [savage] *gardens* [Indian gardens], *and good harbors: the Coast is for the most part, high clayie sandie cliffs. The SeaCoast as you passe, shewes you all along large corne fields, and great troupes of well-proportioned people.*

In the opening chapter of John James Babson's *The History of the Town of Gloucester-Cape Ann including the Town of Rockport*, dated 1860, he wrote:

> *It is not known that any English foot had, previous to 1614, yet pressed our soil; and our Cape still remained without a name. But it was destined this year to be associated with that of a remarkable man, whose wonderful adventures and achievements give to the sober page of history a romantic interest, that, if history were not sometimes stranger than fiction, would*

seem to belong rather to products of the imagination than to the events of real life. Capt. John Smith had already been distinguished in planting and sustaining the southern Colony of Virginia [Jamestown]*; and he now gave his unsurpassed energy, and all the influence he possessed, to the foundation of a settlement on the northern coast. In the employ of some London merchants, he set sail on the 3d of March 1614, with two ships, and forty-five men and boys, for the coast of New England, or, as it was still called, North Virginia. On the 30th of April, they arrived at the Island of Monhegan, on the coast of Maine.*

He continued:

Our plot, was there to take whales, and make trials of a mine of gold and copper. After due trial, this purpose of the expedition was abandoned, and a more profitable occupation was found in trying for fish and furs, which were to be the "last refuge" to secure a saving voyage. While the ships and most of the company were engaged in fishing, Capt. Smith, with a few of his men, in a small boat, sought more congenial employment in ranging the coast and trading with the natives, an employment in which he had had much experience; for he had explored the shores, rivers, and inlets of Chesapeake Bay, a distance of three thousand miles, in an open boat. In this new enterprise, he explored the coast from Penobscot Bay to Cape Cod; within which bounds, according to his own account, he "sounded about twenty-five excellent good harbors." At the latter place he had a skirmish with the Indians; but, within an hour after it occurred, the parties became friends again. Capt. Smith made a map of the territory, and affixed names to its most prominent parts.

Babson goes on to say:

It is not known that Capt. Smith landed on our Cape. The name he gave it was that of a Turkish [actually a Greek maiden], *Lady Tragabigzanda* [Cape Tragabigzanda] *who showed him much kindness while a prisoner in her country. Her name was Charatza and was the Greek mistress of a Turkish nobleman who had gifted her to Smith. Tragabigzanda means "Girl from Trebzone." After his return to England, Prince Charles renamed the cape for his mother, Queen Anna, consort of James I* [Cape Anna] *Queen of Denmark. The only other name given by Smith to any part of our territory was that of the Three Turks' Heads, to the three islands off the head of the Cape; which were so called in memory of an exploit, by which three Turkish champions were successively beheaded by him in single-combat duels.*

Smith's sponsor, Prince Bathory of Transylvania (Romania), presented him with a patent for a coat of arms that exhibited three Turks heads in honor of his victory in combat over the Turkish challengers. These three islands were subsequently named Thacher, Milk and Straitsmouth, situated on the southeast side of the Cape within a mile of its shores.

This description sets the stage for the fascinating story of the settlement of Cape Ann and its surrounding islands. Much has already been written about Thacher Island and the horrific wreck of Anthony Thacher and his family in 1635.

SAMUEL DE CHAMPLAIN

Captain John Smith was not the first explorer to sail past Cape Ann. Captain Bartholomew Gosnold aboard his ship *Concord* from Falmouth, England, passed Cape Ann on his way to Cape Cod on May 14, 1602, while attempting to establish a settlement. Martin Pring aboard the *Speedwell*, in search of sassafras, used as a medicinal herb, passed by in April 1603. Sassafras was in great demand in Europe as a cure for scurvy and syphilis. Captain George Weymouth sailed north from Nantucket to Penobscot Bay in May 1605. By 1606, great interest in colonization, along with fishing and fur trapping, became a priority for the explorer/adventurers from Europe. By November 1620, the Plymouth colony had become the first permanent colony. During the years after 1606, hundreds of fishing vessels established fishing stages from Monhegan Island to Cape Ann.

The French were also exploring North America. In 1606, Samuel de Champlain (1562–1635), the French explorer and cartographer, made his second voyage to Cape Ann and anchored in Gloucester Harbor, naming the area Le Beauport.

There is a sign marker at Rocky Neck in East Gloucester just behind Ten Pound Island dated "1630–1930" that reads, "In September 1606, Samuel de Champlain landed at Rocky Neck in what is now Gloucester Harbor, to caulk his shallop, and made an accurate chart of the harbor which he called Le Beauport." (The shallop was a heavy boat with both sails and oars and a

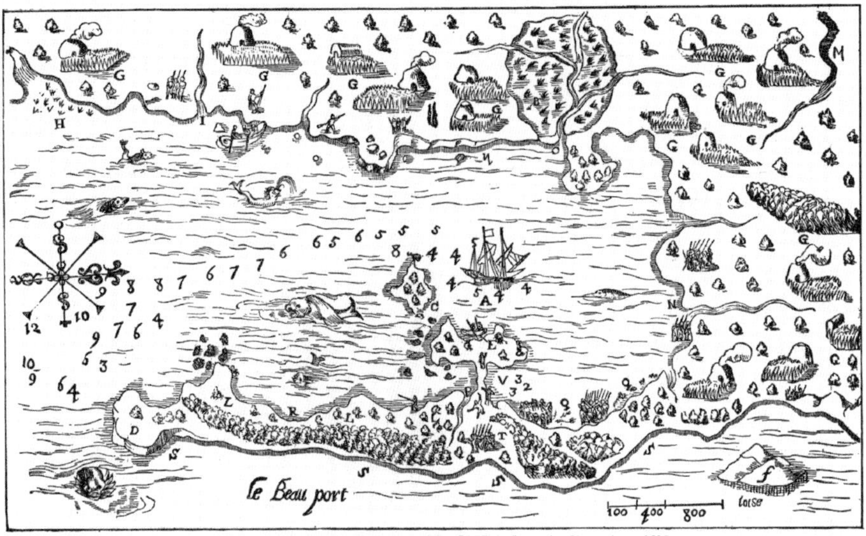

MAP OF GLOUCESTER HARBOR. "LE BEAUPORT." Drawn by Champlain in 1606.

A, Place where their ship was anchored. B, Meadows. C, Little Island. (Ten Pound Island.) D, Rocky Point. (Eastern Point.) E, Rocky Neck. F, Little Rocky Island. (Salt Island.) G, Wigwams of the Savages. H, Little River and meadows. (Brook and marsh at Fresh Water Cove.) I, Brook (at Pavilion Beach.) L, Tongue of plain ground, where there are saffrons, nut-trees and vines. (On Eastern Point.) M, Where the Cape of Islands turn. (The creek at Little Good Harbor.) N, Little River. (Brook near Clay Cove.) O, Little Brook coming from meadows. P, A Brook. (At Oakes' Cove, Rocky Neck.) Q, Troop of savages coming to surprise them. (At Rocky Neck.) R, Sand Beach. (Niles' Beach.) The sea-coast. T, The Sieur de Poutrincourt in ambuscade with seven or eight arquebusiers. V, The Sieur de Champlain perceiving the savages. The figures probably denote the depth of water in metres.

Champlain's map of Le Beauport, created in 1606 upon his visit to Gloucester Harbor while his shallop was being repaired. *CAM.*

shallow draft for navigating shallow waters, such as shoals and sandbars at river mouths. Variations on the shallop were indispensable for all the early explorers of the New England coast.)

Champlain's voyages to America started in 1603, when he first served as a mapmaker on French expeditions, and ended with his death in Quebec, New France, in 1635. He sailed along the northern New England coast to Cape Ann in 1604 and came ashore here in 1605 and 1606. His accounts of meeting the Pawtucket in Whale Cove and Gloucester Harbor indicate friendly, though increasingly wary, encounters.

His first voyage was in 1604, the first authentic record of the landing of white men in this part of Massachusetts. The Pawtucket signaled Champlain's barque from Emerson's Point after it rounded the Cape in 1605. The French were skirting the offshore islands, not sure where to go. The Pawtucket sent up smoke signals at Emerson's Point, which the French saw. The intent was for them to come ashore in Sandy Bay, where archaeological remains suggest a village was located, but after much discussion they anchored eventually in Whale Cove, after which they got up the nerve to make contact. There was mutual ambivalence about making contact. Mariners had been attacked, and Indians had been abducted. The Algonquin had already had Europeans on their coasts for one hundred years or more. His log, *Voyages of Samuel de Champlain 1604–1618*, mentions:

> *Coasting along the shore we perceived smoke upon the beach, whereupon we approached as close as we could, but did not see a single Indian, which made us believe they had fled. The sun was setting, and we were unable to find a place in which to pass the night, because the coast was low and sandy. Steering south to get away from the land that we might anchor, after sailing about two leagues we perceived a cape* [Cape Ann] *on the mainland to the south, one quarter south-east of us at a distance of some six leagues* [a league is about three nautical miles]. *Two leagues to the east we saw three or four rather high islands* [Isle of Shoals]. *The next day* [July 16] *we made our way to the above mentioned cape, where, close to the mainland, are three islands* [these three islands in the vicinity are Straitsmouth, Thacher and Milk Islands] *which are* covered with trees *of different sorts. There is another low island upon which the sea breaks, which extends a little farther out to sea than the others, upon which there are no trees* [likely the Dry Salvages reef]. *We named this place the Cape of Islands* [Cape Ann]. *Near it we caught sight of a canoe in which were five or six Indians, who came towards us, but upon approaching our pinnace, went back to dance upon the beach. I went ashore to visit them, and to give to each a knife and some biscuit, which caused them to dance better than ever.* [This was Whale Cove in present-day Rockport.] *When this was over, I made them understand as well as I could, that they should show me how the coast trended. After I had drawn for them with a charcoal the bay and the Island Cape, where we then were, they pictured for me with the same charcoal another bay which they represented as very large. Here they placed six pebbles at equal intervals, giving me thereby to understand that each one of these marks represented that number of chiefs and tribes….Sailing half a league farther, we observed several savages on a rocky point* [Emerson's Point], *who ran along the shore, dancing as they went, to their companions to inform them of our coming. We anchored near a little island* [Thacher Island] *and sent our canoe with knives and cakes for the savages.*

Today, there is a marker at the corner of South Street and Whale Cove Lane in Rockport that reads, "Due east from here on July 16, 1605, the Sieur de Monts sent Samuel de Champlain ashore to parley

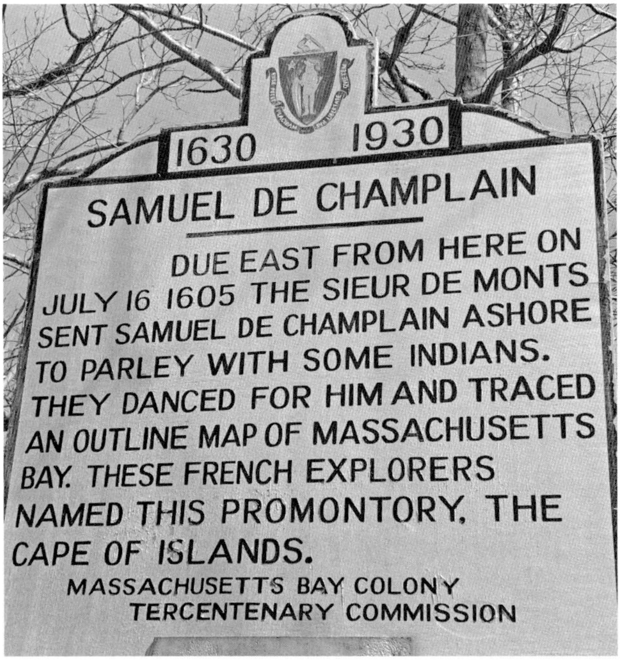

Champlain is memorialized with this sign, indicating his meeting with Indians at Whale Cove in Rockport in 1604. *Author's collection.*

with some Indians. They danced for him and traced an outline map of Massachusetts Bay. These French explorers named this promontory, the Cape of Islands." Sieur de Monts was commander and a French merchant, explorer and colonizer under the reign of King Henry IV of France. Champlain was his cartographer and navigator. King Henry gave De Monts exclusive rights to colonize North America between forty- and sixty-degrees north latitude.

Chapter 4

FISHERMEN AND FISH FLAKES, 1623–1720

Over these early years, fishing vessels from Portugal, Spain and Holland brought back word to Europe of the state of the country and of the abundance of fish in its waters. This induced many of the merchants to conduct fishing voyages to New England, noting that these voyages might be carried on with more advantage if they could be connected with a plantation where agriculture could be pursued. Furs and timber were also considered as added profitable opportunities.

The first to begin this work were some "merchants and other gentlemen about Dorchester" who, after raising the necessary capital, dispatched in 1623 a small ship of fifty tons to set up a fishing voyage and establish the basis of a new colony. Reverend John White of Dorchester, England, attempted to establish a plantation on Cape Ann around the harbor. White and his adventurers worked until 1625 before giving up as the fishing profits never covered their expenses and the agricultural endeavor failed as the area was not conducive to farming. Unfortunately, the fishing season and the planting season coincided, making it difficult to do both with limited manpower. Most men were fishermen and had little interest or experience in farming. The famous Dorchester Company dissolved, and most men returned to England or moved down to the Plymouth Colony.

An interpretive sign erected at Straitsmouth Cove on Marmion Way by Essex National Heritage Commission reads:

> *Straitsmouth Cove Landing—Fishermen from Essex and Ipswich began fishing from this site in the mid-1600s. They soaked their catch*

in brine and sun-dried it for shipment to the Caribbean, England and other faraway destinations. In the early 1800s, the Massachusetts Humane Society established a life-saving station on the west side of the cove which was later operated by the US Coast Guard and is now privately owned.

Fish stages were located at the water's edge, or "land wash," and consisted of an elevated platform on the shore with working tables and sheds at which fish were landed and processed for salting and drying. Traditionally, they are painted with a red ochre paint, although other colors were sometimes used. The stage would operate only for several months during the summer. Stages were found in just about every fishing village along the Atlantic seaboard. They were not infrequently called "camps" because they were where the fishermen would spend the week away from their families—sometimes just down the road and sometimes out on a cape or an island nearer the inshore fishing grounds. They consisted of a wharf connected to (or supporting) a shack where the fishermen slept on the second story and where the ground floor stored much of the fishing tackle and the catch was salted down in barrels or, in the case of cod livers, left in barrels or drums to extrude the cod liver oil. (where the old-timers would sometimes put in a dipper and drink off the vile dark liquid) and some being sold to fish buyers. Centuries later, in the 1950s, 1960s and 1970s, the fish themselves (cod, pollock and herring, although herring were not actually called "fish") and high-value catches like halibut and tuna were still being gutted or filleted on the wharf.

A "fish flake" is a platform built on poles and spread with boughs for drying cod on the foreshore of fishing villages and small coastal towns.

John Babson's oldest son was also named John. He is supposed to have founded the first local commercial fishery on Cape Ann. "Stages" were erected at various times—some under grant from the English king in 1623—but these, like most semi-public enterprises, petered out under absentee ownership. John Babson's fishing headquarters were located at Straitsmouth Cove, where the lifesaving station was located. One of the cottages used as a boardinghouse for employees by the Straitsmouth Inn was built on the foundation cellar of the John Babson fish house, built around 1690. Up to 1700, only one Gloucester fishing vessel had ventured as far east as Cape Sable. This was one of Babson's. After 1700, many schooners of about fifty tons were built and sent to the Grand Banks. By 1740, about 70 of these schooners were operating from Cape Ann. When

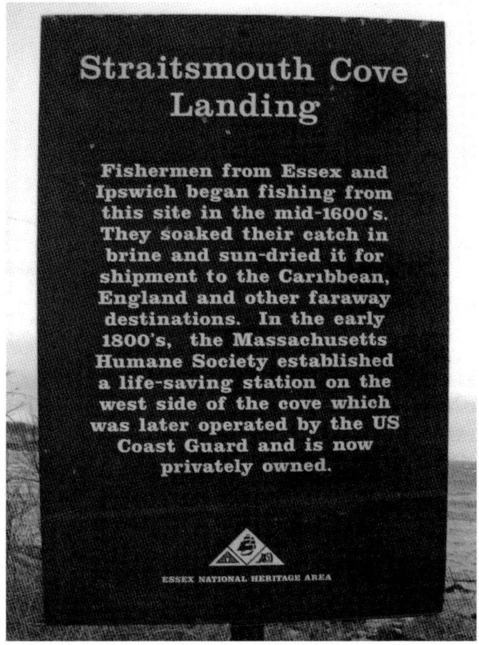

Right: This sign marks the location of the first fishing stages at Straitsmouth Cove in the early 1600s. *Author's collection.*

Below: Example of a fish flake, used to dry fish before it is salted and packed in barrels to be shipped to distant ports. *CAM.*

the Revolution broke out in 1776, 150 vessels aggregating fifty thousand tons were in operation.

James Babson had built a mill on the Alewife Brook in 1642. It was used to grind corn but was primarily a sawmill. Upstream, James Babson had a cooperage (now the Babson Museum) for making barrels and hogsheads from the wood cut at the mill. This cooperage supplied the barrels to fishermen who used them to pack their catch in salt to ship abroad.

The indentation of the coast between Andrews Point and Straitsmouth Point, at the head of the Cape, began to be called Sandy Bay at about the time that the first settlement was made there. The first separate grant of land in that locality was that made to John Babson in 1695, at Straitsmouth, "to sett up fishing upon." It is not known if Babson ever had a home in the area. He sold his land at Straitsmouth in 1721 to Jefford Cogswell, Jacob Perkins and James Smith of Ipswich. These were probably the Chebacco fishermen, known to frequent the shores of the Cape for the purpose of landing and drying their fish.

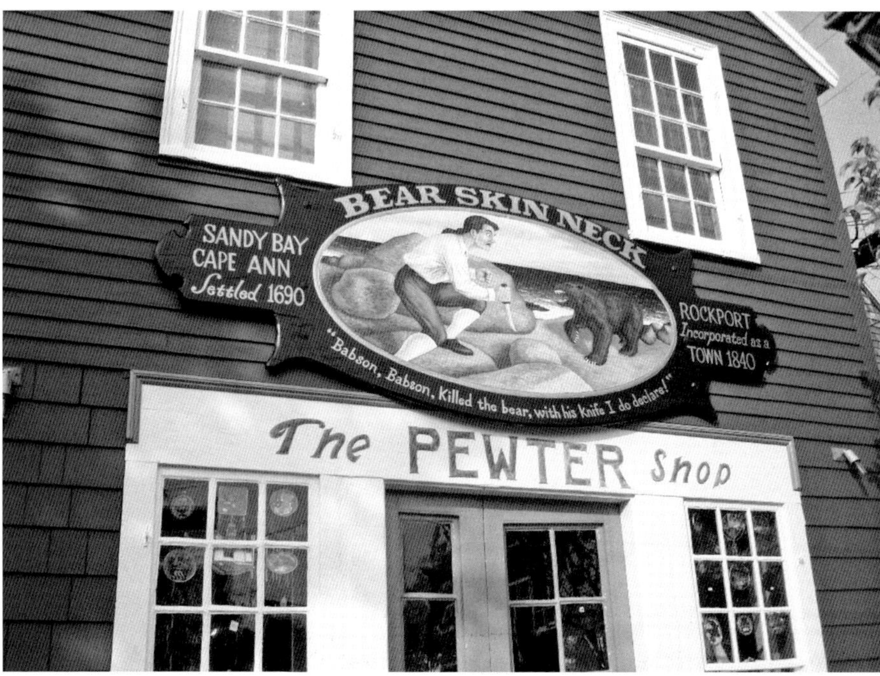

This store sign recalls Ebenezer Babson's killing of a bear and drying the skin, resulting in naming the area Bearskin Neck. *Author's collection.*

The Babson family had a long and varied history around Cape Ann. The famous story of how Bearskin Neck was named in 1713 has been part of the local lore. Roger W. Babson, a descendant of John and Ebenezer, tells his story as follows:

> *Ebenezer Babson, who was then residing at the Babson Farms, saw a bear attack a boy* [his nephew, Henry Witham]. *He immediately attacked the bear to get his attention away from the child but having no gun he permitted the bear to follow him into the water. There, after a terrific struggle, Ebenezer killed the bear with a fish knife* [as depicted in the sign over the front door of the Pewter Shop on Bearskin Neck today].
>
> *He then brought the bear onto the shore, skinned him, and spread the skin on the rocks to dry. Ebenezer died shortly afterwards, presumably at sea, but his nephew Henry Witham, whose life he saved, lived to a ripe old age. Naturally, he often told the story of his rescue, and when people asked how Ebenezer killed the bear, he would reply: "With his knife, I do declare." And hence the little ditty: "Babson, Babson, killed a bear, with his knife, I do declare."*

THE ISLAND'S FIRST OWNERS

The island's present name was given before 1699, when it was granted by the Massachusetts General Court to Captain James Davis, in consideration that he had "been at much charge and expense in the late wars with the French and Indian enemy and spent much time in said service." Its value, in the depreciated currency of 1732, was £225.

Captain James Davis was born in about 1635 and died on May 1, 1715. Davis was appointed by the General Court as ensign to the trainband (civilian militia) in 1681 and, in 1689, received his commission as captain. In 1693, he was "very sickly" in the country service in Sir Edmund Andro's time (Andros was governor of the Dominion of New England who was eventually discredited and sent home to England in 1689), and he received in 1699, from the General Court, a grant of Straitsmouth Island.

He was repeatedly elected to the office of selectman. For eight years, he served the town as its representative. Davis had been married three times. With his first wife, Mehitabel, he had four children—John, born in 1660, and James, born in 1663, were the only two who lived to maturity. With his second wife, Elizabeth Batchelder of Wenham, married in 1666, he had seven children; she died in 1667. By August 1697, he had married his third and last wife, Mary Cook.

In 1795, Joseph Davis of Newburyport owned the island, which had been passed down through the family from Captain James Davis. Joseph and his wife, Rebecca, sold the island to Francis Pool on February 4, 1797, for seventy-six pounds.

Francis Pool was born on June 17, 1729, and married Lois Story on October 19, 1752, at age twenty-three. They went on to have ten children: Captain Ebenezer Pool, born in 1753; Lois, 1756; Moses, 1758; David, 1759; Esther, 1762; Nathan, 1764; Sarah, 1766; Aaron, 1767; and Solomon, 1772. For Francis Jr., we have no birth date, but we know he was killed at the Battle of Bunker Hill on June 17, 1775.

Upon Lois's death, Francis married Margaret Sommes on December 22, 1776, at forty-seven years of age. They went on to produce two more children: Esther, born in 1777, and Francis, born in 1784.

Francis died on June 2, 1804, and his considerable estate included the listing "Straitsmouth Island (so called) $500." His estate was valued at probate on May 10, 1804, at more than $26,000. His son Aaron Pool was executor. Among some of his possessions were a "Dwelling House and garden adjoining and belonging to the same, situated near The Cove (so called) [this was Straitsmouth Cove], valued at $654, two fish houses on bear skin neck, one fourth part of the flake yard held in common with Stephen Pool, and Capt. Ebenezer Pool situated on bear skin neck." He also had two yoke of oxen, eleven cows and their calves, three horses, forty-two sheep, five berths with mooring stones and stumps in Long Cove (today's Rockport Harbor) along with several acres of land and other dwelling houses.

On November 28, 1834, Aaron and Solomon Pool, two of Francis's sons, sold the island for $600 to the collector of the Port of Gloucester, Colonel William Beach, on behalf of the United States, to be used for the placement of the island's first lighthouse by the federal government.

Aaron married Sarah (Sally) Butman on June 22, 1791. He died on January 3, 1845, at seventy-seven. Solomon married Polly Barber Tarr on November 27, 1802, and died on August 5, 1841, at age seventy. All four names appear on the deed.

Opposite: Copy of the original Straitsmouth Island deed dated 1834, sold by Aaron and Solomon Pool to the government to build the island's first lighthouse. *Author's collection.*

102

Deed for Straitmouth Island, Mass.

Know all men by these presents that we Aaron Poole & Solomon Poole of Gloucester in the County of Essex and Commonwealth of Massachusetts, Yeoman, in consideration of six hundred dollars to us paid by Col. William Beach, Collector of the port of Gloucester, for and in behalf of the United States the receipt whereof we do hereby acknowledge do hereby give grant, bargain, sell and convey unto the said United States Straitmouth Island (so called) situated at the North easterly part of said Gloucester. To have and to hold the said granted and bargained premises, with the privileges and appurtenances thereof to the said United States forever, and to their use and behoof forever. And we the said Aaron Poole and Solomon Poole for ourselves, our heirs, executors and administrators do covenant with the United States, that we are lawfully seized in fee of the premises, that they are free of all encumbrances; that we have good right to sell and convey the same to the said United States to hold as aforesaid; and that we will warrant and defend the same to the said United States forever, against the lawful claims and demands of all persons.

And we Sally Pool wife to the said Aaron Pool and Polly Pool wife to the said Solomon Pool, do hereby agree to the above sale and give up all our right of dower and power of thirds in the above granted premises.

In Witness whereof we have hereunto set our hands and seals this twenty seventh day of November eighteen hundred and thirty four

Signed Sealed & delivered in presence of us
George Stevens
Benjamin Pool

Aaron Pool (Seal)
Solomon Pool (Seal)
Sally Pool (Seal)
Polly Pool (Seal)

Essex SS. Nov. 28th 1834 Then the within named Aaron Pool & Solomon Pool personally appeared and acknowledged the within instrument by them subscribed to be their free act and deed

Before me James Goss Justice of the Peace

Essex SS. Received in Registry of Deeds Dec. 1 1834 Recorded Book 279 leaf 68 & examined by

R. H. French Reg

HOW STRAITSMOUTH GOT ITS NAME...MAYBE

The earliest known map that indicated the names of each of the three Turks Heads Islands was created in 1776 by Samuel Holland, Esq., from surveys and soundings and naval observations by Lieutenant Henry Mowat, commander of His Majesty's armed ship *Canceaux*. Subsequent maps by John Mason in 1831 also indicated these islands' current names.

There are no records of how Straitsmouth received its name. It could have been named by local fishermen who had frequented the area since the 1600s to fish and set up fish flakes. Mary Ellen Lepionka related that "Straitsmouth is not an Algonquin place name. It is English and was probably coined by Captain John Smith or possibly the early explorers Martin Pring or Bartholomew Gosnold. I think 'strait mouth' is a pretty good guess at the etymology."

The first official mention of Straitsmouth was when a grant for two or three acres was deeded in 1695 to John Babson "at the strait mouth point to set up fishing upon." You will note that the deed spelled the name in two parts—*strait* and *mouth*, both lower case. This would indicate that the area did not have a name but used the *strait* and *mouth* as a simple location to be noted on the deed. As was the case of Milk Island being named by locals because of its use as a grazing field for milking cows, locals called the area "straight mouth" because it was a straight passage to the mouth of Rockport Harbor.

My hypothesis is that the island got its name from local fishermen who may have referred to its location near the "strait," which is near the "mouth" of Rockport Harbor. Early fishermen were not from the area but came over from Essex and Ipswich, so they may have identified the location by its topographic description as a strait near the mouth of Rockport Harbor (or at the time Long Cove).

Early documents with *strait* separated from *mouth* may indicate that the area had not been named but merely referred to as a geographic location. A strait is defined as a narrow passage of water that connects two large bodies. Many well-known straits exist around the world, such as the Strait of Gibraltar, which connects the Atlantic Ocean with the Mediterranean Sea; the Strait of Magellan, connecting the Atlantic with the Pacific Oceans in the southern tip of South America; or the Bering Strait, which connects the Arctic Ocean with the Bering Sea in the Arctic Circle.

The suffix *mouth* in town names has been used in Great Britain for generations where many coastal towns and cities located near river mouths helped determine that the town was near a river. Towns such as Plymouth,

Bournemouth, Falmouth, Dartmouth and Yarmouth indicate that they are near the exit to the sea from the rivers Plym, Bourne, Fal, Dart and Yare. These rivers vary in length from nineteen to eighty miles.

It must be assumed, then, that Straitsmouth indicates a "strait" that is near the mouth of the harbor, there being no rivers in proximity to the island, although there may have been a stream of some sort back in the 1600s.

Many of the local area towns were named after English counterparts. Names such as Essex, Ipswich, Gloucester, Salem, Boston and Manchester all have sister towns in England, but Straitsmouth does not have a counterpart in England.

The first official use of the name was in the deed written when the island was sold on November 27, 1834, by Aaron and Solomon Pool to Colonel William Beach, collector of the Port of Gloucester, for $600 for the purpose of building a lighthouse station. At that time, Straitsmouth was part of Gloucester—Rockport was not to be a separate town until 1840.

It is also interesting that the actual deed has the spelling as "Straitmouth," without the second *s*. When Stephen Pleasanton, first director of the U.S. Lighthouse Establishment, appointed the first keeper, Benjamin Andrews, on September 1, 1835, the appointment is still spelled without the second *s*. From 1850 and as late as 1866, the spelling appears both ways in the record lists of lighthouses and lighthouse keepers. It isn't until 1892 that the spelling was corrected to Straitsmouth in the U.S. Light-House Board's official records and annual reports.

The island was named to the National Register of Historic Places on June 14, 1987, and ironically was misspelled as "Straightsmouth"—this stands today in the official National Park Service federal government records.

It seems that the federal government has a difficult time properly spelling property it owns. Thacher Island is another example. Often the records indicate the spelling as "Thatcher Island" on many government charts and documents. The correct spelling was without the second *t*, as Anthony Thacher's name is properly spelled. In March 1895, the federal government's U.S. Board of Geographic names published a notice in the *Boston Globe* that Thatcher Island shall have two *t*'s, compounding the problem. In addition, Thacher Island would no longer use the possessive term on all charts and records. After all, it was Anthony Thacher's island from 1636 until his family sold it eighty years later, but the board did not recognize possessive cases in geographic titles and thus it "must be dispensed with."

When it was first mentioned in Anthony Thacher's letter to his brother about the tragedy, he referred to it as "Thacher's Woe."

Chapter 5

FIRST SETTLERS, 1699–1850

The first settlers of Sandy Bay were Richard Tarr, Francis Norwood and John Pool. These three families formed the nucleus of the key settlers. Of course, as years progressed, there were many others, including the Allen and the Davis families.

EBENEZER POOL, 1787-1878

Before we examine the three first families, I should remark on one man who had a significant influence over what we know about the people and history of Rockport and Gloucester. His name was Ebenezer Pool, and he was known for his prodigious interest in recording the events of the day among the various families. He was known as an informal historian of the time. His Pool Papers make up five handwritten volumes archived at the Sandy Bay Historical Society Museum. (A sixth volume contains scraps of notes and ledger books.) They have been digitized and are available to search via the museum's computer. The papers were saved by his youngest son, Howard Franklin Pool (from Ebenezer's second marriage to Jerusha Norwood), who served as custodian of Ebenezer's work. The compilers of *Rockport History of 1888* wrote, "He left a large number of pages of valuable memoranda to which we are all indebted." According to Marshall Swan, "In 1967 the original six volumes of memorabilia assembled between 1820 and 1870 by

Ebenezer Pool were 'rescued' from a trunk in an antique shop and loaned to the Sandy Bay Historical Society and remain as one of the town's most valuable possessions."

Much of the history of Gloucester written by John Babson in 1860 and that of Marshall Swan in his book *Town on Sandy Bay* (1980) uses Pool's information to a large extent. Pool had become a noted antiquarian by 1853. In the *Cape Ann Advertiser* newspaper of Thursday, April 17, 1878, the death notice of Ebenezer noted, "He was remarkable for his wonderfully tenacious memory, going back to events more than 80 years ago, rendering him the chronicler of the town. He had a special gift for tracing and remembering genealogies, and his mind was a treasure-trove of local history."

Ebenezer Pool was born on July 16, 1787. He married Abigail Patch Choate on December 31, 1808, at Gloucester. She died of typhoid in 1825. He then married Jerusha Norwood, daughter of Major Francis Norwood and Lucy Pool, on June 5, 1826, at Gloucester. He died on April 10, 1878, at age ninety. He was the son of Ebenezer Pool (1764–1842) and Sally (Sarah) Grover. He had a brother, William Grover Pool, born on October 9, 1791, who died at age five.

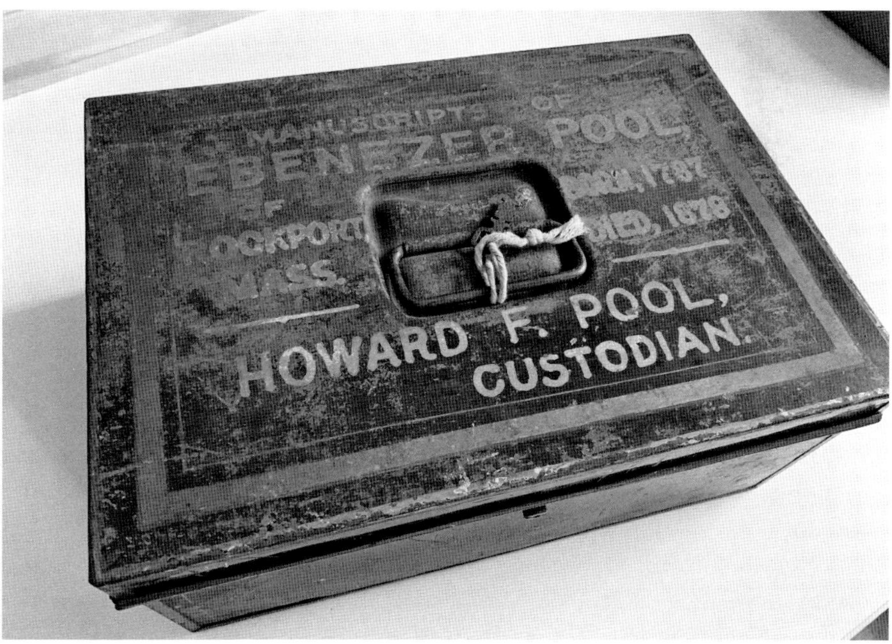

The tin box used to store the original Ebenezer Pool Papers, which his youngest son, Howard Pool, had preserved as his custodian. *Author's collection.*

Portrait of Ebenezer Pool (1787–1878), local antiquarian and recorder of a significant portion of Rockport history. *SBHS.*

Pool served on the 1839 committee tasked with choosing a name for the region seceding from Gloucester. After much deliberation, the committee submitted five options to the people of the new town: East Gloucester, Rockport, Granite, Brest and Cape Ann. With twenty-four votes, the name Rockport narrowly prevailed over Cape Ann, which had twenty-two votes. Eight votes were cast for Brest, and only seven for East Gloucester. Brest is a famous French seaport and was thought to look like Rockport. In his early life, Pool was engaged in coasting (coast-wise shipping) from Maine to Boston, and in later years, his place of business was in a store on Dock Square. He lived in the large white hip-roofed house at no. 10 Dock Square built by his father, Deacon Ebenezer Pool, in 1805 that remains today.

In researching the Pool family, I found no fewer than twelve Ebenezer Pool births listed from 1698 to 1871, making it difficult to accurately trace the Pool family. Most members lived into their eighties. The first Ebenezer Pool (his great-grandfather), born on March 5, 1698 (or 1699), lived in Beverly and then married Elizabeth (Betsy) Norwood on January 30, 1724, daughter of Joshua Norwood, later moving to Sandy Bay. They had ten children, five sons and five daughters. This first Ebenezer Pool was instrumental in building the first wharves of stone and wood near the "Whirlpool" at the Old Harbor and partnering with his brother John Pool and Benjamin Tarr. About 1743, the commoners gave several lots of land on Bearskin Neck to these three men on the condition that they build wharves on the northwest side of the point to create a harbor. (Before 1661, the proprietor of every dwelling house was a "commoner," or entitled to a right in the common land. In 1757, there were 145 claims to these privileges acknowledged as valid. Shortly after 1700, numerous grants of land were voted to newcomers. Several subdivisions of their holdings were made by these commoners. The last apportionment of a woodland was in 1723, when 217 lots within the bounds of the town were disposed of, on terms that every male citizen who had attained his majority receive a certain tract.)

Since fishing and the coastal trade was important, increased docking areas were needed for an expanding fleet. To a petition from Ebenezer and John Pool and Benjamin Tarr, the commoners offered to the parish "Bair Skin Neck So Called with all Common Land that may be spared near Long Cove," together with "the Land and fish Houses stands on Belonging to the Little Boats." They insisted that within three years the fifth parish build a wharf of two hundred feet by thirty feet, "back of the Old Wharff."

Death of Ebenezer Pool

Mr. Ebenezer Pool, an esteemed and venerable citizen, died at his home near Dock Square, on April 10, 1878, at the advanced age of ninety years and nine months. For many years, he was a prominent member of the Baptist church. From early life, he was especially interested in noting important or special events; he was possessed of a very retentive memory and was able to give a ready answer when called on for family genealogy or events that had transpired long before. Mr. Pool was the great-great-grandson of John Pool (born in 1670), who settled in Sandy Bay in 1700—the second permanent settler of the village. He attended school one or more terms in the first schoolhouse in the village; it was built of logs and was located on a part of the now front yard of the Congregational meetinghouse. This schoolhouse was demolished in 1797 or '98. He left a family of nine sons and seven daughters. He had been twice married.

A descendant of the first and second settlers of Sandy Bay, Pool began school in the very first schoolhouse at "ye Cape" and later attended the new Proprietors' School, which opened in 1797. Of his sixteen children, twelve survived him and eleven marched behind his coffin. In Gott's *History of Rockport* (1888), Ebenezer Pool, Esq., is boldly noted on the first page with the words, "Extracts from the Memoranda of Ebenezer Pool Esq.," and recognized as the coauthor of the book.

RICHARD TARR, 1660-1732

In 1697, Richard Tarr had a house at Sandy Bay, on land granted to him by the town on the south side of Davison's Run (today's Mill Brook running through Millbrook Park and into Front Beach—if one stands on Front

Beach, Straitsmouth Light can be seen one mile away). Perhaps he settled there a few years before that date, as it is certain that he was a resident of the town in 1693 and probable that he was here as early as 1690. He came from the west of England in 1660 and settled in Marblehead, where he married Elizabeth. His children comprised seven boys and three girls from which numerous progenies have sprung. Tradition states that Tarr was induced to settle there by the coasters, who, on their visits to the shore to take away wood, occasionally needed help from land. Whatever the inducements, he is distinguished in Rockport history as the first permanent settler at the end of the Cape. His descendants are numerous, and some of them still occupy a portion of the land on which he built a lonely home three centuries ago.

This biographical sketch of "Richard Tarr, the First Settler of Sandy Bay (Rockport)," was written by Ronald David Tarr, a direct descendant, and is reproduced by permission from the Sandy Bay Historical Society:

> *Richard Tarr was born in Wales about 1660. As a young man he sailed across the Atlantic Ocean to seek his fortune in the new world. In 1680 he came to reside in Marblehead MA. Then in 1684, he married a young woman of that town whose first name was Elizabeth* [there is no record of her maiden name]. *In 1685 Richard and his wife moved to Saco, Maine, to live upon 50 acres of upland on the northern side of the Saco River that he had purchased from John Seilye, a local fisherman. There he built a house and took up a life of farming. About this time, two healthy baby boys are born by Elizabeth named John and William. In 1688 Richard sent a petition to Sir Edmund Andros, governor of the English territory of New England. The letter requested that a survey of his land be made. Richard also asked in his petition that his ownership of the vast tract of land be confirmed.*
>
> *When Richard and his family went to church, he always had to sit at the head of the pew with a loaded musket beside him. The Indian situation in the area was dangerous. The fierce Sokokis Indians, members of the Abenaki Indian nation, were on a reign of terror. They tortured and or killed without mercy all the white people they encountered. Even when Richard was out in his fields working, he placed a gun within easy reach. Early in 1689 Richard and his family were forced to leave their beloved home and property for good. Richard felt that the hostile Indians had become too great a danger to his family. The hardy pioneers returned to Marblehead. "In the spring of 1690 that our family came in a pinnace, a small vessel navigated with oars and sails, to Sandy Bay*

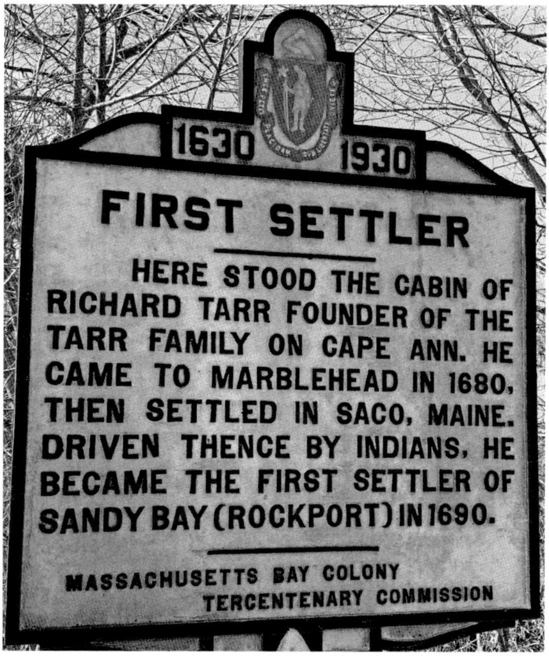

This 1930 tercentenary sign marks the 1690 homestead location of the first settler of Sandy Bay, Richard Tarr. *Author's collection.*

or as it is now known, to Rockport, Massachusetts." Richard had been persuaded to move here by the master of a Gloucester wood coaster. The seamen had told him that this area was uninhabited. Thus, the Tarrs became the first settlers of Sandy Bay and the progenitors of a large family whose members still survive.

Richard claimed the land on the left or the south side of Mill Brook. He then built a house on the brow of the Hill overlooking Front Beach where the lot of number 113 Main Street is today. In 1930 the Massachusetts Bay colony tercentenary commission marked the spot in front of the of the site by erecting a sign with an appropriate inscription.

At the time the Tarr family first settled this most easterly part portion of Cape Ann, the area was practically in unbroken forest. There were no roads and hardly a footpath. Although a fishing port called Gloucester had been founded more than a half a century previous on another part of the Cape, Sandy Bay had scarcely any inhabitants.

On occasion a wood coaster would sail into the Bay to obtain a cargo of lumber with some needy settlement along the Atlantic seaboard. Usually it was in Straitsmouth Cove where conditions were more favorable to beach a vessel, load it from the shore and sail away on the next tide. Richard was often called upon to assist in loading a vessel with wood. He received as payment various "necessary goods of life." The Tarr family had to depend primarily on game for sustenance. He hunted in the dense forests and fished in the nearby fresh and saltwater's. Richard farmed to a small extent as his land was suitable for raising some crops.

A small number of fishermen plied their vocation during the summer months of each year in the ocean waters of Sandy Bay. Seamen came from nearby ports but used the many coves in this area as their fishing headquarters, Straitsmouth being one of the most active. Richard Tarr and his family, though, we're usually left alone by these mariners. The pioneers lived secluded and as it were from the outside world for ten difficult years with their nearest neighbors residing about five miles away.

During this trying period, four more children were born by Elizabeth, Elizabeth 1691, Honour 1693, Richard 1695, Joseph 1698. Then in April of 1697, Richard was allowed by Gloucester to enclose 3 or 4 acres of land where his house stood and to use this property for several years.

Sandy Bay received its second family of year-round residents in April 1700. John Pool, his wife Sarah, and their five children formerly of Beverly, Massachusetts, claimed the land on the right or the north side of Mill Brook. John then built a house in a clearing near the Tarrs. The two pioneer families soon became both near neighbors and good friends. Together with John Pool, Richard Tarr built, owned, and operated the first mill to be located at Sandy Bay. It was situated on a small section of the Tarr estate along the banks of the Mill Brook. Thus, the little body of fresh, running water that spills into the Atlantic Ocean at front beach got its name.

With the passage of years, Richard Tarr eventually was able to blaze a trail through the dense woods extending from his home to the outskirts of Gloucester. When, on June 2, 1707, Gloucester citizens started to lay out a road from their business center to the main part of the village of Sandy Bay or the Fifth Parish of the town, they used as their basis for construction that same crude footpath hacked out of the wilderness by the first settler of Rockport. Part of the remains of this now disused road called the Old Rockport Road can be seen to this day.

After the arrival of the Pools, other settlers began to make their homes in Sandy Bay. Soon a village was formed, in the Fifth Parish of Gloucester came into being.

Richard Tarr donated a portion of his land (one-fifth of an acre) to the newly formed village for use as the communities first graveyard. It is located on a small hill overlooking Front Beach. It is now known as the Old Parish Burying Ground. Here all the early settlers of Sandy Bay

The Old Parish Burying Ground, given to the town by Richard Tarr, who was buried here in 1732 along with many of the early settlers and War of 1812 veterans. *Author's collection.*

are buried, including Richard Tarr. Their tombstones are visible today. In 1930 the Massachusetts Bay Colony Tercentenary Commission erected a sign bearing an inscription at the entrance to the cemetery. The marker commemorates the gift of the land for the burying ground to the town by its first settler.

In 1701, Richard Tarr had ten more acres of land granted to him by Gloucester on the one stipulation that he support an old town pauper named father Arthur Churchill for life. Then, in 1707, Richard again received another land grant for four and one-half acres.

Meanwhile, though, his wife had given birth to 5 more children. Benjamin 1700, Caleb July 4, 1703, Samuel 1706, Abigail 1709, finally Sarah in 1716.

Richard Tarr died of natural causes in the spring of 1732. He was in his late 60s or early 70s at the time of his death. Richard's will had been made on January 7, 1729 but was not proved until June 13,

1732. It made provision for Elizabeth during her widowhood, but it was found later to be inadequate for her support. In later years she had to have outside financial aid.

Most of his property and money was given to his many children. His personal property consisted of three cows, one pair of steers, 3 yearlings, one calf 20 sheep and 6 lambs, one mare and colt, four swine, three beds and furniture saws, augurs and other miscellaneous articles made the total amount come to a little more than ninety-nine pounds. Richard's total final estate was worth about 400 pounds.

Richard Tarr was buried within the old graveyard he had donated to the village many years before. The exact spot where he was laid to his final rest was not precisely known until 1854 when the Town of Rockport decided to honor its first settler. A marble monument costing fifty dollars was erected over his grave in the upper northern corner of the Old Parish Burying Ground on the small hill overlooking Front Beach where it can be seen to this day.

JOHN POOL, 1670–1727

The second settler at Sandy Bay was John Pool. Born in Taunton, England, in 1670, he came to this country in 1690 at the age of twenty. He was engaged as a ship's carpenter with Richard Woodbury in Beverly. He was a master shipbuilder, working on one or more vessels in Ipswich and helping build the first vessel in Gloucester in 1698. In 1700, he married Sarah, the widow of his employer, Richard Woodbury, and removed to Cape Ann, having purchased from John Emerson, son of the minister of the first parish of Gloucester, land on which to settle and build, at a cost of £160. This shows that he was a man of means. His first dwelling was a rude temporary log house. In 1702, he built the first frame house on what is now known as King Street at the corner of Forest Street.

In 1703, we find him drawn as a juryman to attend court in Salem. He built the first sawmill and vessel in Sandy Bay, and in 1710, he furnished several sloop loads of hemlock timber for the building of Long Wharf in Boston. He married his second wife, Sarah Dodge, and later his third, Elizabeth Holmes. After his death, we find his estate valued at $9,000.

The two first settlers, Richard Tarr and John Pool, have suitable memorial tablets raised to their memory near their first homesteads. The extensive

This sign indicates the 1700 home of the second settler of Sandy Bay, John Pool. *Author's collection.*

tract of land that he bought from John Emerson Jr. in 1700 was situated on the north side of Davison's Run, which is today's Mill Brook stream running through Millbrook Park.

We are not sure as to who was the first to join Tarr and Pool at Sandy Bay. In 1715, a John Davis from Ipswich, with his wife and family, moved into town. He may have been the person of the same name, son of Isaac Davis of Falmouth, who in 1734 was living in Gloucester and was about seventy-four years old; Another Davis, Samuel, married Elizabeth, daughter of Richard Tarr, in 1715. It does not appear that he lived at Sandy Bay, but it seems quite certain that other Davises became residents there between 1715 and 1723. This included Captain James Davis who was granted ownership of Straitsmouth Island in 1699.

In 1738, a malignant throat distemper, which prevailed with extraordinary aggression throughout New England for about two years, began its ravages at Sandy Bay and took from the settlers, according to the General Court, "thirty-one of their pleasant children by death." There were then in the place twenty-seven families, containing more than 140 persons. Some of them were of the settlers at Sandy Bay between 1738 and 1754; we know the names but not the date of settlement there.

There is a list in Babson's Gloucester history that contains most of the names of the men who lived in Sandy Bay from 1690 to 1755. This list amounted to fifty-five names, of which there were five Tarrs, nine Pools, three Davises, one Babson and one Norwood.

In 1699, John Day had been given a grant of land that extended from Loblolly Cove to Emmons Point. William Cogswell of Chebacco bought Day's land in 1704 for sixty pounds. He is supposed to have built a house there to accommodate the fishermen of Chebacco.

John Emerson was the original grantor in 1688 and erected a house. His son John had a house on the western end of these premises; this was small and used by his slaves, of which he had several.

In 1701, John Pool Sr. and Thomas Witham had Davison's Run granted them to set up a sawmill. This mill was built on the stream where the old Manning gristmill stood, and afterward John Pool II built a gristmill near the same place. John Pool Sr. died on May 19, 1727, aged fifty-seven years, and was buried on his own land, once owned by Deacon Thomas Giles, at the head of King Street. His stone remained there in 1860 along with part of the stone of one of his wives, of which he had four. All his wives were buried here, and their graves were originally marked by stones.

Mr. Pool's fourth wife, Abigail Ballard, was a widow lady of Rowley. This marriage had a strange twist to it. John Pool had been rejected many times by this lady. He would return often to try to convince her, and he eventually did. She had been so taken by his continued return and persistence that she named her first baby Return to commemorate Pool's romantic actions.

Babson told the story of the exhumation and reinterment of the remains of John Pool and three of his wives (his first wife left him) 150 years later in 1878:

> *A small congregation of men assembled near the residence of Mr. Ephraim Nickerson, corner of Railroad avenue and King street, on the 22d day of October, 1878; their object was to witness the exhumation and re-interment of the remains of John Pool, the second permanent settler of Sandy Bay, and those of three of his wives, which had been buried more than one hundred and fifty years on what was then his own land; but long since this estate had passed out of the possession of his descendants, therefore the call for and the necessity of their removal. It was a matter of special interest to the small number there assembled to know how little the remains of a fellow mortal after so long a burial. The coffins had crumbled so that only a few small fragments remained, a few bits of rusty iron, remains of nails*

John Pool's headstone at the Old Parish Burying Ground. *Author's collection.*

> *and metallic trimmings, some bones, soft and crumbly, with fine fibres of roots and vegetable growth twined closely about, beneath and around every part, winding even into the minutest crevices and embracing every part with their delicate tracery.*

The inscription on the headstone reads: "Here Lyes ye Body of Mr. John Pool, aged about 57 years, Died May ye 19th, 1727." All the remains were placed in a neat box and were reinterred in the old cemetery, and the ancient headstone was placed to mark this last resting place.

The Pool family goes back more than ten generations. Since John's arrival in 1690, the Pool name has been passed on to hundreds of family descendants—one of which, Ebenezer Pool Jr. (1787–1878), was a lighthouse keeper on Straitsmouth from 1852 to 1860. (More about him in the ninth chapter.)

FRANCIS NORWOOD, 1636–1709

Francis Norwood came to Massachusetts from Cheltenham, near Gloucester, England, in 1657 at the age of twenty. He married his wife, Elizabeth Coldham, in 1663 and settled in Gloucester in 1664. Francis Norwood was not the first man to settle at Cape Ann. Small groups of fishermen had settled in Gloucester and the Pools and Tarrs had settled in Sandy Bay, but he was one of the first, along with Joseph Allen, to receive a six-acre grant, from a total of eighty-two then being allotted to all men of Cape Ann. The acceptance of the six acres required the owner to build a house there within six months. The Norwood, the Allen and the Davis families were destined to maintain close business ties and landholdings for many years to come.

Francis and Elizabeth took possession of their land initially at Goose Cove on March 23, 1664, an isolated area of Gloucester, and then grew at a slow pace in the next twenty-five years. While there, the family expanded to ten children—five sons, five daughters. The first son, born in 1664, was named Thomas after Francis Norwood's father, who was lost in battle. He was followed by nine other children: Thomas in 1664, Francis in 1666, Elizabeth in 1668, Mary in 1671, Steven in 1674, Deborah in 1677, Hannah in 1679, Joshua in 1683, Caleb in 1685 and Abigail in 1689.

JOSHUA NORWOOD, 1683–1762 (SON OF FRANCIS)

Francis Norwood continued to live by the motto inscribed on the Norwood heraldic coat of arms: "Never Unready." By the time he died in 1709 at the age of seventy-two, he had acquired 170 acres of Cape Ann land. He left most of his homes and estates to his wife and his children. Francis and Elizabeth's fifth child and second son, Joshua, had married another Elizabeth (Andrews) at the age of twenty-one, after working as crew on boats for five years. From his father's will, Joshua received the gift of 60 acres of Pigeon Cove wilderness on which he and Elizabeth were already settled. Although living surrounded by acres of remote woodland, Joshua and Elizabeth adjusted to their Cape Ann environment. In 1704, Joshua's land (with other owners interspersed) began at the corner fence at the north end of what is now Curtis Street, and it covered the area where Joshua had already established his own home, first known as the "Garrison House" and later on as the "Witch House." The age of this house is unclear, but 1688 is the earliest recorded date for a house with center portion made of logs. This house was built by woodsmen as a refuge from Indians, thus the "Garrison" name, and had squared logs with a fortress overhang. Meanwhile, in 1732, a restless Joshua, having sold his Garrison House to Elias Davis, a prosperous shipping merchant in Gloucester, moved to Attleboro for a period of eight years.

Elias Davis, who bought Joshua's Pigeon Cove house and whose family had already made substantial profits at privateering, may have dispatched Joshua to Attleboro in the interests of both families so they could partake in the active fish, sugar and molasses trade, the latter two used to make rum. Attleboro was located on the major trade route called the Boston Post Road. Tavern keeping was also a profitable business along the New England coast for members of the Norwood family. Taverns were set up in any building available and then used for trading, for decision-making by town officials and often for church services. Whatever the reason for moving, Joshua and Elizabeth returned to Cape Ann in about 1738 and divided their Pigeon Cove acres among their children, having sold the Witch House to Elias Davis before they went to Attleboro.

Joshua purchased more land across Sandy Bay in 1694, behind Straitsmouth Island, and added it to land he already owned there at Gap Head. He took over the land and a log house that he had purchased from John Babson. Log cabins of that day were built in the simplest of styles, with one window and a single door always facing east for the sun. The framework or design of this log cabin was said to have been brought from England. These one-room structures, though dimly lit, often sheltered large families. Within a few years, Joshua and Joshua Jr. claimed their land grants at Straitsmouth, along with Francis (another son of Joshua), as did Joseph Allen.

The point of land called Straitsmouth Point, behind Straitsmouth Island, had been settled by a few landowners a decade earlier and some "nomadic pilgrims" who had traveled north earlier to explore the fishing potential. With the forest and rocky pasture blending into the background and the surf of the Atlantic Ocean at their front door, the settlers fished for cod. In their small boats, they fished from Ipswich on the North Shore all the way to Cape Cod on the South Shore. After long days of fishing, they landed their boat loads of fish at Straitsmouth Cove, where they then split them, removed the backbones and prepared them to be salted, soaked and placed on frames to dry in the open air. Finally, they were shipped in barrels to the Caribbean or to homeports in old England.

Over time, the elder Francis and Elizabeth acquired 180 acres, dividing them among their ten children. Joshua and his father became respected landowners, both men earning the distinguished title of "Gentlemen." The Norwood dynasty was underway on Cape Ann and was soon to be carried on by the sons and daughters of Francis and Elizabeth.

Joshua, a man of many skills, had barely arrived at Straitsmouth to live among the fishermen when he began to make mooring stones, a new industry just established to accommodate the increasing number of fishing vessels. The fishermen/landowners now living there were already set up to make the mooring stones, and Joshua is credited as the first man, along with his son Joshua Jr., to cut the now historic round or square stones for the fishermen, a forerunner of the important industry of quarrying of Cape Ann granite. It is said that the streets of Paris are paved with this same Rockport stone used to make mooring stones. These mooring stones were enormous slabs of granite sliced by hand from pieces of flat ledge that made up the foundation of Cape Ann. Each slab was cut six feet square, ten to fifteen inches thick, with a hole fifteen inches in diameter chip-chiseled out of the center. Into this hole fishermen inserted the entire trunk of an oak tree, chosen for its special size, often as much as twenty feet long, with sections of the roots still attached. The stone was submerged with the tree truck sticking straight up through the hole, allowing the fisherman to tie his boat to the exposed tree trunk, which stood above the waterline, while the roots of the tree settled into the sandy bottom, preventing the mooring stone from moving.

These stones, weighing about two tons, were usually maneuvered onto a skid with the aid of oxen and then hauled to the waterfront. Here they were slipped onto a raft and pulled to a point in Long Cove that the fishermen had chosen to moor his boat. Life on Cape Ann was difficult for Joshua and others living at Straitsmouth in the mid-1700s, and they all joined in the fishing, farming and making of mooring stones to support parents and siblings of their large families. Years later, when Joshua died, he had only land to leave to his heirs, but for a family who descended from near nobility, they were never idle gentry. While the Norwood family acquired acres of land, they also earned a reputation for being hard workers.

Smuggling of commodities such as rum, sugar and molasses became a common practice for pirates spying and scouting the coves of Cape Ann. The Norwood, Allen and Davis families, along with their neighbors haunted by the approach of these unwelcome visitors and constantly on the alert for suspicious movements, were often tolerant of them, as many were British buccaneers from their homeland.

Typical mooring stone used as the sign in front of the Rockport Town Hall. *Author's collection.*

As early as 1717, local fishermen had feared that their waters were being overrun by pirates ready to capture their cargo or their ships. Joshua Norwood, when in his eighties, was said to have made a habit of watching the pirates whenever they came ashore near Straitsmouth, usually at night, noting their activities and stealthy movements. Sometimes Cape Ann mariners were as merciless as the pirates in finding ways to make a profit. Rumors of pirates seeking shelter in their many hidden coves raised constant alarm among the local settlers. The pirates who scouted the Cape Ann shoreline were said to have their own secret harbors, with Gully Point and Gap Cove behind Straitsmouth Island among their favorites. Joshua died on September 25, 1762, in his eightieth year.

Caleb Norwood, 1736–1814 (Son of Joshua)

Caleb, the youngest son of Joshua and Elizabeth, was two years old when the family established themselves at the Straitsmouth District on Cape Ann. By the time he was ten, Caleb had learned how to fish off the rocks and from a small boat. He talked in terms the fisherman used, and every style of boat and sail were familiar to him. His father taught him how to clear the gravelly surface of rocks and pebbles and how to plant seed to vary the family's diet of cod and other food from the ocean. He knew his neighbors and worked with them as brothers. Caleb knew that a "gundalow" was a barge or scow with a small sail designed to collect the harvest of salt hay to fertilize their meager soil, so rocky and so close to the shore that even their farms were dependent on the harvest of the sea.

Caleb was nicknamed "Red Cap" because of the military cap he wore as an act of defiance against the British, and his brother Joshua Jr. continued to live near Gap Cove. At age twenty-four, Caleb married another Elizabeth (Grover), but after ten years of marriage and bearing five children, Elizabeth died. Caleb was left with the care of five young children and lost no time in finding another wife in Ipswich. Within three months, Caleb had married Jeshura Story in 1770. Two more children were soon added to the family: Francis, known as "Major," born in 1771, and William, born three years later.

In 1772, the year following the report of his discovery of gold (see the sixth chapter), Caleb moved his cabin, built in 1740, from Straitsmouth to the edge of Sandy Bay Harbor. It's not known if he moved it by water or by a cart along a dirt road one mile away. In any case, he placed the log house on his own land at the corner of what is now Mount Pleasant Street and Atlantic Avenue.

In 1708, Peter Bennett was having a log cabin built near Pebblestone Beach, at the west of the Witham or Grover pond (today's Henry's Pond). He moved away soon afterward to Georgetown, Maine.

Peter Emmons, at the same time, lived near Loblolly Cove in a log cabin. The point took its name from him (now called Emerson's Point). He and Peter Bennett are said to have pastured cows on Milk Island, hence the name. Nothing more is known of Peter Emmons.

In 1743 or thereabouts, the second settlement took place at Gap Cove. Joshua Norwood settled there in 1694, supposedly occupying the house previously occupied by John Babson at the bend of the cove, having a grant of three or four acres at the cove as Babson had before him. Here old Joshua died; some years afterward, his sons Joshua and Caleb built the other two houses, Joshua on the west in the pasture and Caleb on the northwest point. Babson mentioned in his 1860 *History of Gloucester* that "the cellars are now to be seen." Babson went on to say:

> *Caleb was the one who, found the pot of gold on Mr. Francis Pool's land, before the war of 1776, at the south end of the gully. It was uncoined*

The 1680 log cabin of Joshua Norwood (father of Caleb) was moved from Straitsmouth Point to Atlantic Avenue and is now a private home. *Author's collection.*

gold in one-ounce pieces. He is said to have shared it with Mr. Pool; the value is not known but thought to have been high. Mr. Jabez Tarr, the old Revolutionary soldier, said he saw one piece of the gold in ingot. Tradition further says that the ingots were exchanged for depreciated paper money, turned into the state treasury as securities on interest which brought 1.10% per day until redeemed by the state. The second wife of Norwood is said to have had a ring made of this gold. In those early times, money diggers were often engaged in exploring wild and solitary places on the coast. They came here from a distance, with their mineral rods, and generally went away in the night. It is not known that any more money was found. In later times, people have visited the place where the pot of money is said to have been found. These mysterious meetings were generally held in secret in the night and no person was allowed to speak during the digging lest, if they got hold of the bale of the pot, it should escape out of their hands, it was wont to do through some mysterious agency. There also is an old tale that some one hundred years ago two young women coming up from the shore, having been saved from a wreck, fell into the Gully and were killed.

In 1743, business was increasing, and the fishermen needed a more convenient harbor for larger craft and safety than just Long Cove. Ebenezer Pool, John Pool and Benjamin Tarr petitioned for a grant to build a wharf at the "Whirlpool," so named because the small harbor on the backside of today's Lumber Wharf did not have the stone breakwater it does today and the action of the tides, currents and winds would create a whirlpool in that small, shallow cove. This was the first wharf built of timber and stone and the first pier in Sandy Bay. Each of these persons had a storage lot granted him, near the Whirlpool. In 1746, Ebenezer Pool had a lot to the southwest of the first grant for a wharf, the first wharf being just inside the present old wharf. Mr. Pool built a wharf on his grant, about where the middle wharf now stands. These two wharves made quite a safe dock while they stood, leaving an entrance of about seventy-five feet. In 1811, the Sandy Bay Pier Company was established. In 1832, it acquired land at Long Cove, and in 1836–40, it built the breakwater that went from the end of Bearskin Neck toward the Headlands, finally forming a genuine harbor.

Mr. Benjamin Tarr, if half of the stories were true, was the Goliath of his day, for Babson related "that he lifted an anchor weighing eight hundred pounds and logs which a yoke of oxen could hardly draw and performed other feats of strength."

SALT

Salt was a needed commodity and hard to come by. From 1775 on, for several years, salt was very scarce and therefore very dear; because of this, many of the fish were imperfectly cured.

A man by the name of Gallup came to Folly Cove and set up boiling saltwater for making salt, which the Chebacco fishermen purchased. He built a wharf of logs that the tide soon washed away, hence the name Gallup's Folly, which then became Folly Cove.

The manufacture of salt by the evaporation of seawater is an ancient industry, in vogue in 1690. Fires were kept burning under large boilers day and night, and the water gradually evaporated, leaving a residue of pure salt.

To save salt, Mr. Caleb Norwood introduced the practice of salting fish in hogsheads and found it more economical. His son William was the first person to fit out a vessel to salt mackerel in casks on board of the vessel, for packing and exportation.

Salt has played a prominent role in the European exploration of North America and subsequent American as well as Canadian history. The first Native Americans "discovered" by Europeans in the Caribbean were harvesting sea salt on St. Maarten. When the major European fishing fleets discovered the Grand Banks of Newfoundland at the end of the fifteenth century, the Portuguese and Spanish fleets used the "wet" method of salting their fish onboard, while the French and English fleets used the "dry" or "shore" salting method of drying their catch on racks onshore. This was the method used by the early fishermen, who set up their fish flakes at the Gap near Straitsmouth. Due to this early food processing, French and British fishermen became the first European inhabitants of North America since the Vikings a half century earlier. Had it not been for the practice of salting fish, Europeans might have confined their fishing to the coasts of Europe and delayed "discovery" of the New World.

Reports from Onondaga, New York, in 1654 indicated that the Onondaga Indians made salt by boiling brine from salt springs. Colonial Americans were making salt by boiling brine in iron kettles during the time that the U.S. Constitution was being drafted. By the Civil War, thousands of workers were producing more than 225,000 short tons of salt by boiling brine. Historians believe that Native Americans produced salt from salt springs more than five hundred years before the arrival of Europeans. Salt produced by boiling brine supplied the War of 1812.

The novel *Captains Courageous* by Rudyard Kipling, published in 1897, accurately describes the lives of the "salt bankers," as they sailed from Gloucester to the Grand Banks of Newfoundland in search of cod. Owing to the length of their journeys and the lack of refrigeration and freezing, most of the cod catch was salted at sea. The salt cod fishery was in every respect an industry. Salt was imported from as far away as Sicily and England. The fish were marketed worldwide and particularly in countries such as Surinam, which had earlier participated in the "triangle trade" of slaves/rum/salt fish.

The Cape Ann Museum has some magnificent glass plate negatives by famed photographer Martha Hale Harvey of the giant three-masted salt barques delivering tons of salt at the numerous salt docks around Gloucester Harbor.

Chapter 6

PIRATES, PRIVATEERS AND PYRATES, 1500–1725

THE GOLDEN AGE OF PIRACY

As long as people have taken to the sea, there have been pirates. Every culture and country whose ships have dipped a paddle into the salty brine or raised the sail to harness the wind has contended with what the Greek poet Homer called "sea-wolves raiding at will, who risk their lives to plunder other men." Captain John Smith, the controversial English explorer and one of the founders of the Jamestown colony in Virginia, had it right when he remarked, "As in all lands where there are many people, there are some thieves, so in all seas much frequented, there are some pyrates." Almost two thousand years before Smith, Roman historian and statesman Dio Cassius wisely observed, "There was never a time when piracy was not practiced, nor may it cease so long as the nature of mankind remains the same," so stated Eric Dolan in the introduction to his book *Black Flags, Blue Waters*, published in 2018.

Captain John Smith often mentioned "pyrates" in his memoirs during his world travels in Turkey, Greece and Europe in the 1500s. Smith himself was known to be a pirate. Before he sailed for the Virginia wilderness and had his famous encounter with Pocahontas, Smith had been a mercenary, a pirate, a slave and a mutineer, according to the late historian Philip J. Barbour of the Institute of Early American History and Culture in Williamsburg, Virginia, perhaps the foremost John Smith scholar. In one episode, after being shipwrecked on an island off Cannes and saved by French captain La Roche's crew, he joined their ranks. Like many French captains who plied the Mediterranean, La Roche engaged in both trade and piracy. Smith's four months as a pirate with La Roche made him a rich man.

Smith idolized Sir Francis Drake, who sailed around the world and plundered gold from Spain. He too gained the reputation of a pirate, which seemed to impress Smith at an early age.

Sir Francis Drake was famous for his circumnavigation of the world from 1577 to 1580. His was the first English expedition to achieve this goal, second only to Ferdinand Magellan's voyage accomplishing the same feat for Spain between 1519 and 1522. The motivation behind Drake's voyage, however, was not navigational glory but money. His secret orders from Elizabeth I were to plunder Spanish positions in the Pacific, even though England and Spain were then nominally at peace. Elizabeth had a profound resentment of the Spanish and especially against her brother-in-law, King Philip. Her plan was to attack Spanish towns and ships along the western coast of South America. Drake soon amassed a fortune in silver and gold, his most impressive conquest being the ship *Nuestra Sonora de la Concepcion*, which carried a fortune in gold bars, silver coins, silver bullion and jewels. Drake's ship, the *Golden Hind*, returned in triumph to England, arriving in Plymouth Harbor on September 26, 1580. Philip II labeled Drake a pirate, which undoubtedly, he was. His countrymen simply viewed him as a privateer and a hero. Two hundred years later, the poet Samuel Taylor Coleridge's observed, "No man is a pirate unless his contemporaries agreed to call him so."

Privateering was a frequent occupation of many fishermen and local mariners here in North America. Privateering was encouraged by ship owners of the time, as it allowed vessels to attack enemy ships of the day and either take their cargo or the entire ship and, many times, the crew. A privateer is a private person or ship that engages in maritime warfare under a commission of war. Two kinds of privateering permits were granted by the authorities. One allowed the use of privately owned vessels only as a privateer or ship of war. The other commission, also known as a letter of marque, empowers the person to carry on all forms of hostility permissible at sea by the usages of war, including attacking foreign vessels and taking them as prizes. The proceeds were divided by the privateer sponsors, shipowners, captains and crew. Most privateers were simply pirating. William Kidd (Captain Kidd), for instance, began as a legitimate British privateer but was later hanged for piracy. Kidd had made his way from his home in Scotland to the Caribbean and eventually up the coast of New England, and he was put behind bars in Boston in 1699 and posed no threat at this time to Cape Ann fishermen.

The years from 1700 to 1725 were considered the golden age of piracy. Piracy had been an active occurrence around the world since the fifteenth century. In New England, piracy was often encouraged by the populace, as pirates supplied goods and currency that was hard to come by. Seaport communities were reluctant to testify against mariners, not for fear of retribution but rather fear of losing their best benefactors. Piracy was a cozy business to sailor and merchant and everyone in between.

THE *SQUIRREL*

In April 1724, one pirate ship captured several vessels off Cape Cod and succeeded in taking two Gloucester fishermen as captives. Since this incident, more seizures had taken place, sometimes with cargoes of salt taken, but often a cargo of fish resold for a higher price. In the spring of 1724, the first known confrontation with pirates occurred at Goose Cove, in full sight of the Francis Norwood house. Construction of a new vessel, the *Squirrel*, was all but finished, and the crew was preparing for its trial run when a pirate gang, long feared for their frequent harassment of Gloucester ships, boarded in stealth and commanded the crew to complete the carpentry under guard. The pirates were led by John Phillips, a noted pirate, who the next day abandoned his own vessel and went on board the *Squirrel*.

Phillips had been harassing New England waters for the past two years. During their first season, they had taken thirty-four vessels, which they looted, killing or maltreating crews. The owners, however, resolved not to give up to the pirates' seizure without a struggle. On the seventeenth, Captain Andrew Harraden, with John Philmore and six other prisoners, made plans to forcibly recapture their vessel. They devised a courageous plan to await his signal at noon on the eighteenth, when the pirates might be momentarily idle and off guard, and then, with their carpenter's tools, overpower their captives and take back their ship. Edward Cheeseman, one of the men who planned the recapture, seized John Nott, the second in command of the pirates, while he was walking the deck and threw him overboard. Harraden struck down Phillips with an adze, and another man dispatched Burrell, the boatswain, with a broad axe; the others fell on James Sparks, the gunner, whom they also threw overboard.

Not only did the bold plan succeed, but Captain Andrew Harraden also sailed the *Squirrel* back into Goose Cove with the heads of the pirate leader John Phillips and Burrell swinging from the sloop's masthead. John Nott, a pirate almost as notorious and feared as the well-known Captain Kidd, was hanging from a tree on nearby Hangman's Island, so named from the fact that two of the bodies of the dead pirates were suspended from gibbets erected in the center of the island in the Annisquam River. The other members of the crew were brought to Boston and were arraigned before the Admiralty Court on May 11. Thirteen were acquitted as forced men. John Rose and William White were found guilty of piracy and sentenced to be hanged on June 2. White's body was suspended in irons in Boston Harbor on Bird Island, which disappeared in 1946 under the newly created Logan Airport runways.

Babson noted that "the people of Gloucester commenced privateering; but at first only on a small scale, making use of their fishing boats for the purpose." In June 1775, the British sloop of war *Falcon*, under command of Captain Lindsey, fired on the town and tried to set it on fire. They captured several Gloucester men, mortally wounding two. In November, the privateer *Lee*, commanded by Captain Manly, brought into Gloucester Harbor the ship *Nancy* from London, bound to Boston; an ordnance ship, it had on board a great quantity of small arms and ammunition, besides cannons, as well as a large brass mortar. These articles were greatly needed by General George Washington. The mortar, once delivered to Cambridge, was pronounced the "noblest piece of ordnance ever landed in America" and christened the "Congress."

The first vessel that put to sea from Gloucester on a privateering mission was a fishing schooner, the *Britannia*. Refitted in the summer of 1776, it was renamed *Warren* after the Patriot General Joseph Warren, a physician who died in the Battle of Bunker Hill in June 1775. It had eight guns, all old but serviceable. During the month of September, it captured three prizes, the first was the *Picary* of 400 tons, the next a brig of 120 tons and the last a ship of 500 tons called the *Sarah and Elizabeth*.

Five small-armed vessels, commissioned by the state, made Gloucester Harbor their homeport. They cruised by day and captured many vessels. Another privateer that set out in 1777 was the schooner *Speedwell*, with Philemon Haskell as captain. It captured three fishing brigs—*George*, *Dolphin* and *Phenix*—each with a cargo of fish and salt. Salt was greatly needed at the time and fetched a very high price.

On April 5, 1779, the privateer ship *General Starks* sailed on its third cruise from Gloucester. It had a crew of 135 men and boys and mounted eighteen guns. It was commanded by Captain Coas and battled with the British brig *Porcupine* of fourteen guns. It struck to the *General Starks* without firing a gun. It went on to take at least six more vessels as it sailed to Bilbao, Spain.

Babson related stories of no fewer than fourteen brigs and other privateers that operated out of Gloucester from 1776 until the end of the Revolutionary War. Once the war was over and there was little call for privateering, many men turned to piracy as jobs for skilled mariners disappeared.

PIRATE JOHN QUELCH

John Quelch began as a privateer in 1704, working as second in command for Captain Daniel Plowman aboard the eighty-ton brigantine *Charles* out of Marblehead. Lieutenant Quelch was a London-born mariner; Plowman was hired as a privateer and awarded a letter of marque by Massachusetts governor Joseph Dudley, commissioned to attack French and Spanish ships off the coast of Newfoundland and Arcadia. Before leaving Marblehead, the crew mutinied and locked Plowman, who was deathly ill at the time, in his cabin and later threw him overboard once at sea. No one knows if he had died or the mutineers simply threw him into the sea. Quelch was voted captain by the crew of forty-three men. Instead of heading toward Canada, they sailed south to Brazil, where they plundered nine Portuguese ships. They never told their benefactors or sponsors about this drastic change of plans. Many of these ships were gold ships returning to Portugal from the gold mines of Brazil.

The *Charles* returned with large amounts of sugar, hides, cloth, guns, gold dust and coins. The loot's total value was more than £10,000 pounds (some £1 million today) before their capture; legend says that some of the crew buried gold on Star Island off the coast of New Hampshire. Many of the crew sailed to Isle au Haut to join with pirate and former privateer Thomas Larimore, who was captured shortly afterward. Before leaving Cape Ann, where most of the crew had escaped, it was rumored that the men buried gold on either Straitsmouth or Gully Point near Straitsmouth Cove.

Quelch and his men had earlier taken the gold coins and gold dust to a famous silversmith in Boston by the name of John Noyes and convinced him to allow Quelch himself to use his crucible to melt down his stolen treasure. Quelch had two reasons to do this: to erase any trace of a connection to

This is a silhouetted sail plan of a brigantine like the *Charles*, used by the pirate John Quelch. *Author's collection.*

Portuguese gold and silver and to make it easy to transport the now more compact gold bars or ingots.

Quelch and six of his men were arrested in Marblehead, but thirty-four other crew members were still at large. Some headed to Rhode Island and others to Long Island. Others were sighted on Cape Ann in Gloucester and farther north around Sandy Bay. Some of them were planning to join the well-known privateer Captain Thomas Larrimore on his *Larrimore Galley* and make their escape with him. A posse of more than forty men of the local militia from Gloucester, Beverly and Manchester told the county sheriff via an express rider from Cape Ann that the previous night between nine o'clock and eleven o'clock "pirates, double-armed" had been "seen in a lone house there." Could this have been the old log cabin once owned by John Babson near Straitsmouth Cove? Could the pirates have buried their gold in the rocks of Gully Point?

On June 9, the militia men boarded the fishing shallop *Trial* to sail after Larrimore, who was reported to be heading for the Isle of Shoals, about twenty-five miles to the north. As the *Trial* approached the *Larrimore Galley*, with the militia men hiding low on the deck, Larrimore himself realized that he was outnumbered and surrendered. Forty-five ounces of gold dust was found. Seven of Quelch's men were returned to Salem and

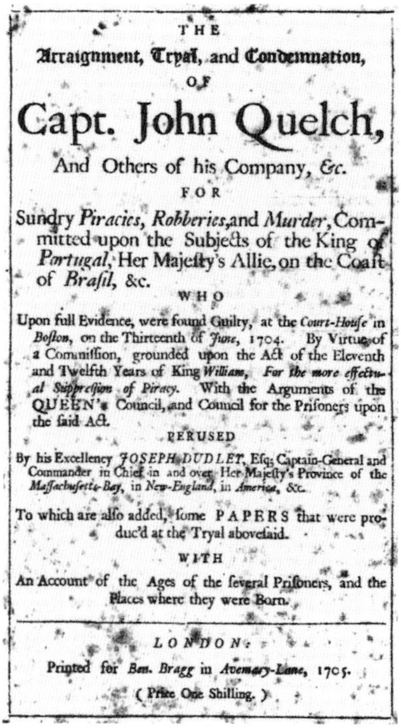

THE

Arraignment, Tryal, and Condemnation,

OF

Capt. John Quelch,

And Others of his Company, &c.

FOR

Sundry *Piracies, Robberies,* and *Murder*, Committed upon the Subjects of the King of *Portugal*, Her Majesty's Allie, on the Coast of *Brasil*, &c.

WHO

Upon full Evidence, were found Guilty, at the *Court-House* in *Boston*, on the Thirteenth of *June*, 1704. By Virtue of a Commission, grounded upon the Act of the Eleventh and Twelfth Years of King *William*, *For the more effectual Suppression of Piracy.* With the Arguments of the QUEEN's Council, and Council for the Prisoners upon the said Act.

PERUSED

By his Excellency *JOSEPH DUDLEY*, Esq; Captain-General and Commander in Chief in and over Her Majesty's Province of the *Massachusetts-Bay*, in *New-England*, in *America*, &c.

To which are also added, some PAPERS that were produc'd at the Tryal abovesaid.

WITH

An Account of the Ages of the several Prisoners, and the Places where they were Born.

LONDON:

Printed for *Ben. Bragg* in *Avemary-Lane*, 1705.

(Price One Shilling.)

Cover of *The Arraignment, Tryal, and Condemnation of Capt. John Quelch And Others of His Company*, published in London in 1705. *Library of Congress.*

jailed. In the end, only about half of Quelch's men were captured; the rest simply disappeared along with their cut of the loot.

Quelch was later hanged, as the letter of marque did not cover Portuguese ships, Portugal being an ally of England and Queen Anne. Twenty of the crew were tried, and six were found guilty, including Quelch. On Friday, June 30, 1704, the six pirates, Quelch among them, were marched through Boston to Scarlet's Wharf. Upon reaching the gallows, the minister (reportedly Cotton Mather) gave the pirates a long and fervent sermon. All showed repentance except for Quelch, who stepped up while holding his hat and bowed to spectators, warning them, "They should take care how they brought Money into New England to be hanged for it." Their bodies were buried between the tide marks. Quelch was only thirty-eight. He had only been a pirate for one year but reputedly was one of the most successful pirates of his time, having captured more treasure than Captain Kidd and the notorious Edward Teach, also known as Blackbeard. Captain Kidd had been imprisoned in Boston and eventually was sent to London for trial in 1701. He was found guilty and hanged in chains at Tilbury Point on the lower Thames in May 1701. Quelch set out on his pirating adventures just two years later in 1703.

In Eric Dolan's book, he stated that "much of the treasure was never recovered. A considerable amount was taken by the crew members who escaped justice, and even those who didn't likely offloaded some of their loot before being captured." Could some of this missing gold have been part of Caleb Norwood's discovery?

Norwood's Gold

The gold rumor was reawakened in 1771 when stories began to be spread that Caleb Norwood, who lived near Straitsmouth, had found a cache of pirate gold bars. Caleb and his brother Joshua Jr. lived at Straitsmouth Point near Gap Cove in 1771.

It was believed that Caleb unearthed a container of gold "ingots"—pieces in the form of gold bars—at the south end of Gully Cove, a familiar and favorite hideout for pirates. Norwood had kept the story secret, but it was known that he only shared his find with his neighbor, Francis Pool, who owned the land on which the gold was believed to have been found. Later, Caleb was known to have given £1,000 each to his two sons Stephen and John, who were preparing to move to Maine. Where did Caleb get that kind of money? He was not a rich man and lived in a primitive log cabin near Straitsmouth. Later that year, he moved the cabin to Long Cove (now Rockport Harbor). Caleb also gave significant sums to the Revolutionary War efforts. Jabez Tarr, a citizen preparing to serve in the Sandy Bay Militia, stated in a note, "I saw a piece of the gold ingot." Francis Pool also gave money to the war effort for guns and to pay the militia members, as records show him receiving large interest payments on bonds issued by the state in 1777.

In their book *Fish, Timber, Granite and Gold*, Peter Bergholtz and Donald Dawson did further research to substantiate their claim that Caleb Norwood indeed discovered this treasure. They found papers in the diary of historian Ebenezer Pool at the Sandy Bay Historical Society library that read, "[T]he money find was not made public but was of many thousands value." They also came across the papers of historian John White Marshall dated 1772 in the SBHS archives that stated, "We have good reason to believe that Caleb Norwood found buried, near the South gully at Gully Point, from 7000 to 10,000 pounds [British currency] in gold." Marshall, by the way, was able to know of the gold firsthand because he and Caleb's son, Caleb Jr., at one time shared in the first Sandy Bay fish business, established in 1837. Since currency of the time was difficult to convert to today's valuation, conversion rates between dollars and British pounds varied widely by month and region. The Bergholtz and Dawson book made a rough valuation of between $400,000 and $700,000 of gold found.

It is also known that Francis Pool had bought significant amounts of bonds to help pay for arms and pay soldiers' wages for the Revolutionary War. Pool had enlisted in John Rowe's Cape Ann Company and gave his life at the Battle of Bunker Hill on June 17, 1775.

Ebenezer Pool in the fourth volume of his papers, recounted the story of the gold: "Caleb Norwood born 1736 built a timber one story house to the east of the gully on his 4 acre lot at gap head, he later moved it up to the south of long cove [the present harbor]…where it still stands today. In the year 1771 or ab't that time he found a pot of ounce pieces [some $10,000] of uncoined gold to the S.W. of his house in land of Francis Pool in the cart way a few rods S. of the Gully, he gave Francis a small part of it, [he] being owner of the land."

Finally, Caleb lived near Gully Point and Straitsmouth and had an excellent vantage point from his log cabin window, able to observe any furtive movements at Straitsmouth Cove. There were many pirates and privateers along the Massachusetts coast during much of the 1700s. Caleb soon began to invest in more land, but he also moved to a larger house to replace his log cabin. His neighbors would wonder where the money came from for such purchases.

Caleb Norwood eventually bought the thirty-five acres known as Allen's Head for £160 in 1772. This area was originally named by Captain John Smith as "Ye Faire Headlands." Later, the land was bought by Joseph Allen, a well-to-do merchant from Gloucester in 1721. Allen was the same man who had owned Thacher Island to pasture his oxen from 1725 to 1771. It became known as Allen's Head. Once Norwood purchased it, it became Norwood's Head. Today, it is simply known as the Headlands.

Down through the years, the stories of hidden treasures in Straitsmouth and the Headlands have persisted. Many digging parties have been conducted in great secrecy in the dead of night. Rumors have floated around of pirate ghosts appearing. These stories have always been told locally. The Norwoods built houses—where did they get the money? It is known that Frederick Norwood, owner of merchant ships, sailed around the world, even to Russia. It is probable that the Norwoods had large interests in merchant ships as well as in fishing; it has been reported that the family possesses curios and works of art, bought from all parts of the world.

Some years ago, when a cellar was being dug near the site of Joshua Norwood's log cabin at Straitsmouth, buried china came to light, and a perfectly preserved finely cut statuette of lava was discovered, giving rise to more rumors of pirate gold. Legends of pirate gold and buried treasure are connected everywhere in the irregular, rock-bound coast of Massachusetts North Shore, the Isles of Shoals and the coast of Maine. But nowhere does the mirage of these tales shine more brightly than on the Rockport end of old Cape Ann.

Cannons still in place at Stage Fort Park overlooking Gloucester Harbor named Fort Conant in memory of Roger Conant, one of the first settlers in 1623. *Author's collection.*

Caleb Norwood and Francis Pool had once been reported as partners in a privateering venture. Could they have acquired their wealth this way as opposed to discovering pirate gold?

Rumors of Norseman from AD 1004, the first daring old English sea dogs of the fifteenth century, and later Captain John Smith's adventures all gave rise to yarns of buried treasure. The natural harbors, the secluded coves, the silence of the primeval forest that then covered the Cape and the many springs of "good water" made it an enticing place for men of the high seas to gather. At that time, the dark chasms, hidden rocky shoals, headlands and unexpected whirlpools made dangerous sailing for all ships and times of storm on poorly charted waters. Many a storm-disabled prize was unloaded and relieved of its cargo by the farsighted fisherman, privateers and pirates of the Cape.

Piracy continued into the 1860s, when the Confederate barque *Tacony* began taking fishing schooners from Gloucester off Georges Bank in 1863. It destroyed the *Marengo*, *Ripple*, *Elizabeth Ann*, *Rufus Choate*, *Ann* and *Wanderer*, which were the finest in the fleet, valued at between $2,000 and $5,000 each.

The *Tacony* was eventually burned to the waterline by its captain, but not before more Gloucester fishing schooners had been captured or destroyed. These actions caused the citizens of Gloucester to appropriate $3,000 for defenses of the harbor at a town meeting held on July 13. Immediate action was taken to erect fortifications at Eastern Point, and an earthwork fort was built and manned. Defenses were thrown up at a commanding position on Stage Fort and named Fort Conant in memory of the early settler, Roger Conant. The cannons are still in place today.

Chapter 7

SHIPWRECKS, REEFS, SHOALS AND LEDGES

STRAITSMOUTH, "A DANGEROUS SPOT IN THE OCEAN"

This entire area around Cape Ann is extremely hazardous to shipping, beginning with the harbor entrance near Avery's Ledge and the Salvages, where Anthony Thacher lost his family in 1635 and was eventually blown by the hurricane and washed up on Thacher Island. Thacher Island, then known as "Thacher's Woe," was awarded to him by the General Court of Massachusetts. Anthony Thacher was awarded forty marks by the General Court of Massachusetts "toward his greate losses." In 1636, Governor John Winthrop and the court granted Thacher "the small island at the head of Cape Ann, which he was preserved from shipwreck as his proper inheritance."

Charts of Cape Ann show that there are six lighthouses, each within six miles of one another, all in a twenty-square-mile area. On these charts can be seen numerous ledges and rocks, including the Londoner Reef and Thacher, Straitsmouth and Milk Islands. Rocks such as Oakes Rock, Twelve Foot Rock, Dodge Rock, Bartlett Rock, Mitchell Rock, Harbor Rock and Pigeon Rock, adding to this the frequent nor'easters and shallow water, combine to make the area one of the most dangerous along the Massachusetts coast. It is ironic that the remnants of the Sandy Bay Harbor of Refuge breakwater that was planned to safeguard mariners and their vessels and had never been completed is itself one of the most hazardous boating areas on Cape Ann.

Just in the two-square-mile area near Rockport and Straitsmouth Island, there are three lighthouses, a lifesaving station, numerous buoys and day-markers, all in proximity.

A few statistics are important. In the *United States Life-Saving Service Annual Report* for 1881, Davis Neck Life-Saving Station in Annisquam reported 23 disasters, 6 vessels lost and 122 lives saved. The 1894 issue of *New England* magazine noted that "in this area for the past 20 years 147 wrecks were reported and 560 partial disasters."

The thirty acres of Straitsmouth Island are surrounded by reefs, shoals and ledges that can be lethal to mariners. The lighthouse that stands on Straitsmouth today is, in fact, the third to have been built there. Following is a sampling of some of the more notable wrecks that have occurred near Straitsmouth.

OCEAN REPORTER, OCTOBER 2011

The most recent wreck on the southeastern edge of Straitsmouth involved local fisherman Captain Bill Lee, who ran his steel-hulled fishing boat *Ocean Reporter* onto the ledge at high tide, only to see it heel over as the tide ebbed, leaving it high and dry. During the night, the tide returned and flooded the bilge room, permanently sinking his entire vessel. The author and a film

The fishing vessel *Ocean Reporter* was wrecked on the ledge near Straitsmouth Island in 2011. *Author's collection.*

crew from National Geographic Network aboard Lee's boat at the time were returning from Thacher Island and had to be rescued by lobstermen who witnessed the disaster. Rockport's harbormasters and the U.S. Coast Guard tried pulling the craft off the ledge but were unable to do so even after all extra weight was removed. By 7:00 a.m. the next morning, the vessel had turned over and sunk in three fathoms of water. Later, Captain Lee dived on the wreck to salvage some expensive underwater camera equipment only to find that the boat, as Lee reported, "was squashed like a pancake" by the severe waves crashing on the ledge. The townspeople rallied and set up a fundraising drive to help Lee get back on his feet and buy him a new *Ocean Reporter.*

USS *Grouse*, September 1963

September 1963 saw the wooden minesweeper and navy training vessel USS *Grouse* hit the Little Savages reef within view of Straitsmouth. It had been built and commissioned on October 25, 1943. It was originally the *YMS-321* and served in Pearl Harbor in 1944. It was renamed USS *Grouse* and used as a training vessel throughout the '50s and '60s.

The minesweeper USS *Grouse* was burned by the navy when it could not be removed from the Little Salvages reef in 1963. *Associated Press.*

In late September 1963, it departed Portsmouth on what was to be a two-week training exercise. At 1:15 a.m. on Saturday morning, September 21, while approaching the headlands of Cape Ann, the *Grouse* suddenly struck a submerged rocky outcrop. Its commander, Allen E. McCartney, had a crew of thirty-six sailors, most of whom were serving their annual Naval Reserve duty time. The commander tried to back his craft off the reef, but the tide was ebbing, pinning the boat to the reef.

Several attempts were made to remove the 136-foot vessel by three navy tugs up from Boston. Unable to free it, the navy doused it with gasoline and a flare was fired into the wooden ship to set it aflame. Within minutes, it was a burning inferno. Five officers and thirty-one crewmen had been removed with no injuries. Today, the only remaining trace is its engine block, which can be seen just below the surface at low tide.

CHELSEA, FEBRUARY 10, 1957

The small coastal tanker *Chelsea* was once a familiar sight along the North Shore, delivering fuel to various harbors. On February 10, 1957, after loading up with six thousand barrels of no. 2 light fuel oil, it was consigned to Newington, New Hampshire. Its captain, Keith Beale, steamed out of Boston on the journey north. Although this was his first command, the skipper felt comfortable enough to hand over the helm at around 10:30 a.m. to his chief mate and retire below. One hour later, all aboard were stunned when a sudden impact brought the tanker to a halt. They had struck a submerged section of the Sandy Bay breakwater. The mate had decided to cut between the Dry Salvages and Straitsmouth Island, following the channel commonly used by the commercial fishing fleet of Cape Ann. Captain Beale raced on deck to ascertain the tanker's condition. He found that it was perched on rocks with an eighty-foot gash running along its bow toward amidships.

The tide was falling. The captain sent out a distress message to the Coast Guard. The cutter *Evergreen* responded that it was attending to another tanker wreck farther down the coast at Little Misery Island in Salem Bay—the *Franco Lisi* had run aground the day before in a dense fog. Once the cutter had pulled the *Lisi* safely off the island, it would be free to respond. The *Evergreen* finally pulled alongside the tanker nearly six hours later, just as the incoming tide began to free it from its perch. Before the *Evergreen* arrived and shortly after the *Chelsea* struck, a thirty-six-foot Coast Guard motor lifeboat had reached the scene and evacuated all but Captain Beale from the tanker. At low tide, the crew was returned to the wreck so the captain could temporarily patch the gash in its hull. By the time the cutter had arrived, this effort had failed, and all that could be done was for the lifeboat to pass two large towing hawsers over with the intent of pulling it into Gloucester for repairs. The tanker's pumps were manned to keep up with the influx of seawater. However, as the *Evergreen* towed the leaking tanker toward the harbor, water began to inundate the *Chelsea*'s hull and the pumps could not keep up.

Up off Loblolly Cove, the stricken vessel began to settle rapidly below the waves. The 36-foot lifeboat sprang into action alongside the *Chelsea*, taking Captain Beale and his crew off just as the decks were awash. The *Chelsea* sank on its side but slid along the granite formation and finally landed upright on the ocean floor. The impact caused its hull to split midships. Its oil cargo released to the surface but wasn't considered a hazard to the immediate coastline due to the strong northeast winds and the light consistency of the fuel. It was built in Bath, Maine, in 1919, and measured 169 feet long, with a 30-foot beam and a gross tonnage of 556. Today, the remains of the *Chelsea* lie on the ocean floor off Loblolly Cove. It has deteriorated over the years, but this site has become one of Cape Ann's most visited shipwrecks. Given the relatively shallow and clear water, the steel hulk has attracted scuba divers from throughout the Northeast.

CHARLES S. HAIGHT, APRIL 2, 1946

The *Charles S. Haight* was one of nearly 2,700 Liberty ships built during World War II to deliver much-needed supplies to the Allied armies. After the war, they were put into service helping to restore the devastated economies of the war-torn European nations. Such was the mission of the *Haight*, which was to sail to Newport, England, with a cargo of coal in early 1946. Once it arrived, the cargo was offloaded, and on March 20, it headed back to the States in ballast, destined for Boston. On the night of April 1, the 7,198-ton *Haight* was battling whistling winds from the southeast, with snow squalls drastically limiting visibility. Captain Joseph Mamo, the *Haight*'s thirty-six-year-old skipper, found that his ship at best could barely make headway. Shortly after midnight, having been blown off course, the 422-foot *Haight* struck fast to a rock ledge known as the Flat Ground off Rockport inside

The liberty ship *Charles S. Haight* lies on its side on Flat Ground Ledge in 1946 and was scrapped where it lay. *SBHS.*

Straitsmouth Island. It was reported by Richard Young of Detroit that he was at the wheel and the vessel slid up on the ledge at 12:07 a.m. The course was 215, in a southwesterly direction. Other crew members said a fishing vessel's light was mistaken for the lighthouse on Thacher's.

Keeper Austin Beal of the south tower of the twin lighthouses at Thacher's said he went off watch at midnight but saw no lights approaching. Visibility was poor, and a strong southeast wind was blowing. Although the damage was extensive, with the no. 5 hold breached, the captain believed that because of its double hull construction it was still possible to salvage the ship, especially because the winds and seas had abated. The navy tug *Moreno* and the Coast Guard tug *Ojibwa* arrived on scene from Boston. At 7:30 a.m., the picket boat from Straitsmouth Island Coast Guard Station, with BMIc Frank Jandrlich in command, approached the side of the wreck to stand by. Jandrlich reported that he saw no distress signals and doubted that any could be seen because of the thick weather. He was told by Captain Mamo that the ship was leaking but holding fast and that the only fear was that the cold ocean waters would flood the boilers, setting off an explosion. As a safety measure, the captain ordered his men off the ship. At 3:00 p.m., two lifeboats and a picket boat were able to take aboard all twenty-nine crewmen and transfer them to the *Ojibwa*. Captain Mamo and eight officers remained on board to render assistance with the salvage efforts.

Owners of the ship contracted a salvage firm and sent a huge salvage tug, the *Resolute*. Coast Guard transferred the responsibility of the salvage to the private company. At 9:00 a.m. on April 3, an attempt was made to remove the captain and its six officers as a storm blew in with significant waves. Shortly before 10:10 a.m., the Coast Guard lifeboat was sent out, battling huge swells the whole way. Once on scene, many attempts were made for each man while the lifeboat risked destruction alongside the ship. Only one man at the time could climb down the swaying rope ladder as the winds twisted and turned the hapless officers. After a complete all-day assessment, it was determined that the *Haight* had split in two up to the main decks and that any efforts to refloat it were futile. It was decided to scrap it where it lay. Whatever was left, the ocean would consume over the next few months. Portions of its engines are still visible at low tide, and the immediate sea floor is scattered with its remains. The bow section ended up halfway between where the engines are and the Sandy Bay breakwater. According to members of the crew, the ship was not equipped with radar.

THE USS *WARRINGTON*, MAY 31, 1916

On the evening of May 31, 1916, the navy destroyer USS *Warrington* was conducting sea trials off Cape Ann. It was part of the North Atlantic fleet, which made annual summertime visits to Sandy Bay in Rockport. At approximately 7:30 p.m., the *Warrenton* was proceeding at an estimated twenty knots when it suddenly crashed into the submerged Sandy Bay breakwater off Rockport. Unknown to Lieutenant Dortch, commander of the *Warrenton*, this resulted in a large dent in the bow, but more disturbing was the extensive damage to the starboard aft section, where water was flowing into the hull at a rapid rate. The impact also snapped the struts holding the propeller shafts, causing them to hang down in a precarious position. The blades were heavily damaged as well. The accident was spotted by two of the fleet battleships, the USS *New York* and the USS *Delaware*, anchored nearby. They immediately lowered their boats and raced to the scene. The damage was concentrated at the stern, and its watertight bulkheads were holding firm; the pumps were able to keep up with the water.

The *Warrington* was a destroyer with a complement of seven officers and seventy sailors, who worked through the night making temporary repairs until daylight, when they were able to make up enough steam to limp to Boston Light. They were met by a navy tugboat, which assisted them to the Charlestown Navy Yard. It was estimated that at least six weeks would be needed before it could return to service.

This was not the *Warrington*'s first brush with disaster. In December 1911, while cruising off the Virginia Capes at night, it was struck by a schooner that ripped thirty feet off her stern. The engine room flooded, cutting off power and leaving it dead in the water. It was forced to anchor seventeen miles offshore and wait for relief. Once again, its watertight bulkheads saved it, and it was towed to port for repairs. It patrolled the northeast coast of the United States and was later sent to Europe to help deal with the U-boat menace off the British Isles. It was decommissioned in 1920 as part of the navy's downsizing program after the war. The *Warrenton* had a gross tonnage of 742 and was an oil burning steam propulsion vessel with a maximum speed of thirty knots. Its full complement was eighty-nine officers and men. The submerged breakwater remains controversial even to this day, as many more victims have been claimed by this ambitious government project gone awry.

WILLIAM H. YERKES JR., 1912

The Boston tug *William H. Yerkes Jr.* was well off its course. Captained by Edward Perkins, it was bound from Boston to Portsmouth, New Hampshire, for a tow struck the ledge at Straitsmouth Point and was ashore and leaking badly. The grounding occurred at about 3:00 a.m. in an extremely dangerous position. Although there was no wind, there was a heavy sea and the tug was pounded badly, opening the seams and filling with water. Captain Perkins and his crew remained on board until daylight, when they rowed ashore and telephoned to the owners in Boston. The lifesaving crew from Gap Head Station went out to the grounded tug at daylight and stood by. At 11:30 a.m., the tug *Leader* arrived to render assistance and found the stranded craft on its beam ends. The *William H. Yerkes Jr.* was built in 1901 and was now a total loss.

DUDLEY PRAY, FEBRUARY 13, 1908

Captain Charles Bearse and his lifesaving crew at the Straitsmouth Station were watching the seas on February 13, 1908. Suddenly they saw the large steam tugboat *Dudley Pray* approaching Straitsmouth Island, having returned from dropping two barges off at Newburyport and returning to Boston. The *Pray* was more than one hundred feet long and 215 tons—one of the most formidable tugboats on the eastern seaboard. Captain Coffin, skipper of the *Dudley Pray*, decided to cut close to the shoreline of Rockport since there was a smooth sea and good visibility. The tugboat slammed into the submerged southerly section of the Sandy Bay breakwater. Captain Coffin immediately threw the helm into reverse, hoping to pry the craft off its perch.

Unfortunately, the tide was falling, and the tug was stuck fast. To lighten the vessel, the crew and the lifesavers together threw all its pig iron ballast and most of its bunker coal overboard. Three additional tugs were sent up from Boston to try to drag it off and set it free. The crew stationed below decks noticed three large holes punched into the *Pray*'s hull by the jagged rocks underneath. The steam pumps being used to drain the vessel couldn't keep up with the influx, and the salvage efforts were put on hold as the tide receded. Finally, they believed the hulk would be light enough to salvage. Unfortunately, a southwest gale commenced on Saturday and lasted through the weekend. By Monday morning, the *Dudley Pray* had slipped off the ledge and sunk in deeper water. Only the smokestack and flagpole were visible.

On Tuesday morning, the tugboat *Orion* arrived at Rockport with a large wrecking lighter, *Trilby*, in tow. The salvage master believed that the submerged wreck could still be saved. Its machinery was removed, and divers could patch the holes in its hull. Eventually, it was unable to be saved because its hull began to break apart. The tugboat *Dudley Pray* had been built in Boston in 1890. Its estimated value was $50,000 but was insured for only $40,000.

SCHOONER *HATTIE PAIGE*, MARCH 7, 1899

On February 23, 1899, with a cargo of granite consigned to New York, the *Hattie Paige*, a coastal schooner, set sail from Greens Landing, Maine. Buffeted by storms, it ducked into Pemaquid, Maine, during a heavy northwest gale with a split foresail. It continued south, again running into high winds and seas, forcing it to seek shelter in both Portland, Maine, and Portsmouth, New Hampshire. Eventually, it limped into Rockport harbor. Captain B.D. Kelly, skipper of the *Paige*, came to safe anchorage—or so he thought. The *Hattie Paige* would remain at this location through the weekend while its sails were being repaired in Gloucester. By 5:00 a.m. the next morning, its cables had parted, with the wind driving it broadside toward the rocky outcrop known as Knowlton's Point. The captain skillfully maneuvered the craft into a somewhat softer landing at Rockport's Back Beach in view of Straitsmouth.

However, when the schooner struck the beach, a combination of its heavy cargo and the battering of the building seas resulted in the loss of its keel, which created huge gaps in its hull allowing seawater to flow freely in. The Humane Society Station in Rockport had been alerted, and the station's Captain Parsons ordered a team of heavy horses hitched to the mortar carriage while the lifesavers sped to the scene. Once abreast of the wreck site, the mortar gun was positioned opposite the schooner and a projectile was launched over the vessel's rigging. This was retrieved by the *Paige*'s crew and secured to the highest location on the mast. The lifesavers next reeled over the breeches buoy, and one by one, all seven crewmen were brought to the beach.

Once safely ashore, the men were brought to the home of old Mr. Eben Knowlton and given dry clothing and warm food after having suffered severely from exposure. The Rockport lifesaving crew was later commended for the heroism shown in saving the crew of the wrecked schooner. The

The granite coastal schooner *Hattie Paige* was beached at Back Beach in Rockport in view of Straitsmouth in 1899, a total loss. *SBHS*.

Hattie Paige was built in Bridgeton, New Jersey, in 1867 and homeported in Yarmouth, Massachusetts. It was 115 feet long, with a gross tonnage of 297. It was a complete loss and unfortunately uninsured. The *Hattie Paige* quarter board is on display at the Sandy Bay Historical Society Museum in Rockport. A recently built home at 41 Granite Street, in the vicinity of Back Beach and Knowlton's Point, has been named "Hattie Paige" by its owners in memory of the daring rescue of the crew.

LETTIE S. REED, SEPTEMBER 23, 1884

As reported in the *Boston Globe* of September 23, 1884:

> *The schooner* Lettie S. Reed *was battered against the rocks of Straitsmouth Island, having started from Provincetown Sunday afternoon on a seining trip off Rockport, where the fleet had gathered for the past few days. She was one of about 100 of the finest fishermen in the world, which had made such a grand display in the Bay for the past few days. They had nearly all of them secured good fares and were either lying at anchor dressing their fish or going to market, last night when the northeast gales struck them. All anchors were weighed, and all vessels got away without damage. The Reed weighed anchor with the rest, but as she neared the wreck of the schooner* Starlight *on Avery's Rock, they found it necessary to come about in order to give the wreck a wide berth. This made one more hitch necessary, and then tacking the second time near Straitsmouth Island, Captain Emery thinks he must have become entangled among some of the fishermen's nets as her head way was unaccountably stopped.*
>
> *Before headway could be regained, she struck heavily upon the Straitsmouth Point. Nothing could then be done but save life, as the wind was increasing in fury, and the sea breaking over her. To land was a very difficult matter, as the rock is shelfing. The seine boat was brought into requisition, and though loaded with a heavy seine the crew got her to windward and succeeded in boarding her and clearing the wreck without accident. They landed safely at Rockport. The vessel still holds together but must quickly break up, as she cannot stand the force of such a heavy sea. The schooner* Starlight, *ashore on Avery's Rock split in two at 11:00 o'clock and sunk out of sight.* Starlight *had wrecked upon Avery's the day before on September 22nd, she was carrying a cargo of coal.*

SAMUEL GILMAN, MARCH 27, 1883

It was reported in the *Boston Weekly Globe* on March 27, 1883, that the schooner *Samuel Gilman* of Boston, Captain M.H. Nickerson, bound for Rockport in ballast after a cargo of paving stones, went ashore on Straitsmouth Point at one o'clock:

> *A heavy gale was blowing, and the tremendous seas made a clean breach over the ill-fated vessel. The crew could be plainly seen from the shore clinging to the rigging, but the undertow was so heavy that the lifeboat did not dare to venture out. For five hours the wretched sailors hung there, wet to the skin, amid piercing blasts and grasping the icy ropes with numbed fingers in full sight of the helpless crowd on shore. At last a big wave, more powerful than the rest, picked the vessel up as if it had been an eggshell and landed her so high on the beach that the men could, with difficulty, get ashore. Straitsmouth, where they are now, is four miles from the mainland, and there is no way of reaching them tonight. The vessel will be a total loss. The escape of the men was miraculous.*

Three months later, the schooner *Clarabel* wrecked on Avery's Ledge, also with a load of paving stones.

MENEMON SANFORD, AUGUST 2, 1862

The coastal steamer *Menemon Sanford* was one of the larger vessels operating along the New England coast during the summer of 1862. The 245-foot steamer was built in New York City in 1854 and used that port as its main operating base. During the summer months, its regular service routes took it from Boston to the resort ports along the Maine coastline. On August 2, 1862, the *Sanford* was cruising along on the final leg of a trip from Bangor to Boston. On board the steamer that early Friday morning were about two hundred passengers. As the steamboat approached Cape Ann, dense fog rolled in. Although the mist obscured all the navigational beacons, the captain of the *Sanford* kept its speed at twelve knots, a rather fast clip for these conditions.

Anthony Thacher and his family were aboard the pinnace *Watch and Wait* when it fetched up on the Dry Salvages in 1635. *Dorothy Snow Bicknell.*

At about 3:00 a.m., as the skipper strained to make out the lights of Thacher and Straitsmouth Islands, the steamer smashed headlong into the rocky outcrop of the Salvages. The steamer was stuck hard and fast, but the influx of the seawater into its bow was found to be minimal as the fog began to lift. Rescue craft from Rockport began to arrive on the scene. In small groups, the two hundred passengers were taken off and safely landed in Rockport. A special train was ordered by the steamboat company, and soon all were conveyed to Boston. The *Stanford* had been one mile off course and had struck on the notorious Salvages reef some two miles to the north of Straitsmouth Island. Once again, efforts were made to lighten the steamer. Workmen aboard the salvage lighter began stripping it of all its fixtures, as well as its heavy equipment. Attempts were made to pull it off, but newspapers of the time failed to mention whether they were ever successful. Its remains can still be seen below the waters off the Salvages to this day.

I would like to thank author Captain Raymond H. Bates Jr. for allowing me to use some of the stories from his fabulously informative book *Shipwrecks North of Boston, Vol. 2: Cape Ann* regarding the wrecks of the USS *Grouse*, *Chelsea*, *Charles S. Haight*, *Hattie Paige*, USS *Warrington*, *Dudley Pray* and *Menemon Sanford*, all of which had wrecked within view of Straitsmouth.

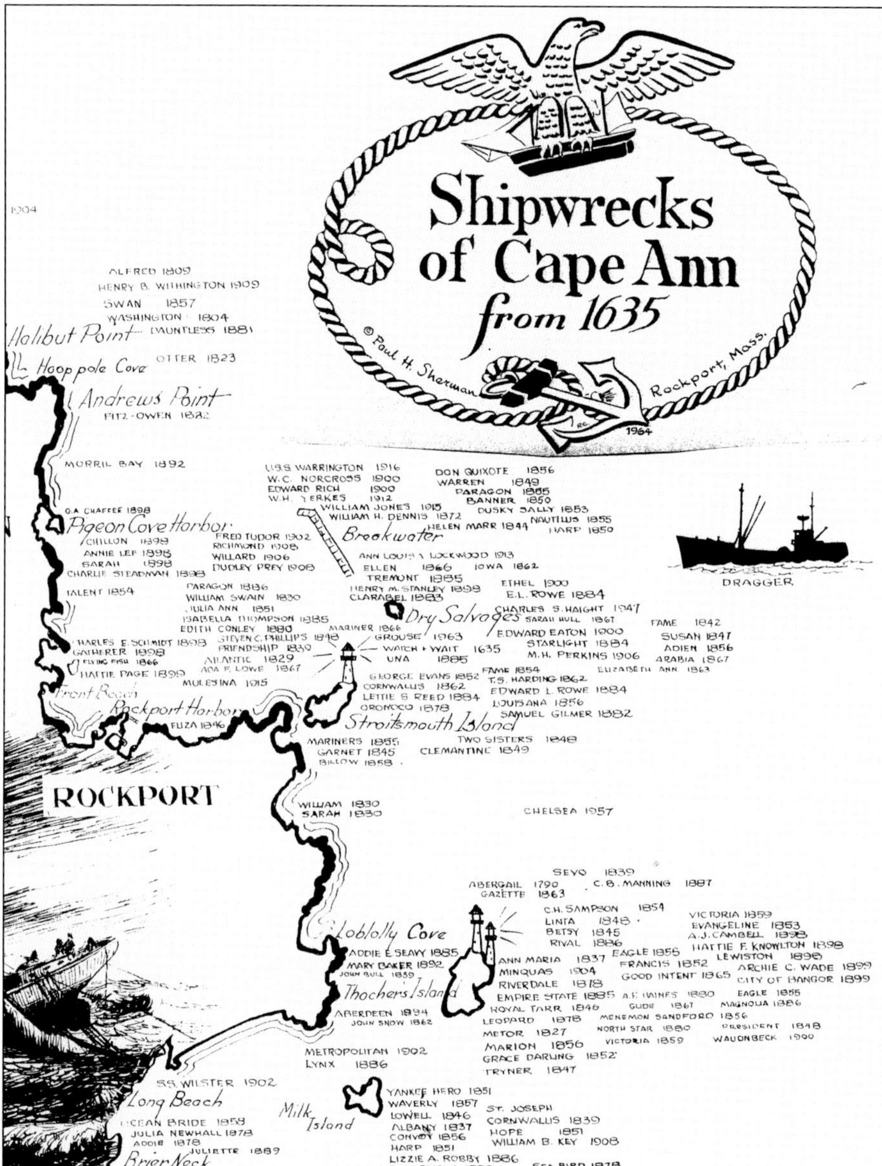

Paul Sherman's chart of the hundreds of wrecks reported around Cape Ann from 1635. *Author's collection.*

Ebenezer Pool's papers reported many other wrecks in the Straitsmouth Island area, a sampling of which are listed here:

- 1830: The schooner *Sarah*, with Charles Rowe as master, ran onto Old Garden beach.
- 1844: The schooner *Helen Mar*, with a cargo of lime, ran onto Flat Ground Rocks just north of Straitsmouth.
- 1848: Thomas Parsons, skipper, ran his fishing vessel onto Milk Island in the fog.
- 1852: The schooner *George Evans* from Maine ran ashore in the Gap with a load of lumber.
- 1855: The boat *Mariner* ran ashore near Gap Cove on December 25.
- 1856: The schooner *Louisiana* from Newburyport—heading to Philadelphia with a cargo of five hundred barrels of mackerel, potatoes and apples—ran onto Straitsmouth Island and then was driven off and sunk north of the Gap.
- 1898: The schooner *Sarah* ran on Avery's Rock but was able to get off.

Of course, the most famous wreck occurred on August 14, 1635, on the Dry Salvages, involving the pinnace *Watch and Wait*; Anthony Thacher, his family of seven, his cousin Reverend John Avery and his family of eleven and a crew of five, a total of twenty-one, were drowned, leaving only Anthony and his wife, Elizabeth, as survivors swept with the wreckage to Thacher Island.

It was recorded by the federal government in the mid-1800s that more than seventy thousand vessels passed by Sandy Bay annually. Paul H. Sherman of Rockport did a massive research project recording shipwrecks around Cape Ann and the North Shore. He produced a detailed chart of the area entitled *Shipwrecks of Cape Ann from 1635* in 1964, noting the vessels, dates and approximate locations. His research reveals more than 450 wrecks in the area around Cape Ann. In his listings, we find 68 around Thacher, 14 around the Londoner, 54 around Straitsmouth (Salvages, Avery's Ledge and Gap Cove) and another 32 near Milk Island, Loblolly and Whale Coves. Is there any wonder why there are three lighthouses, more than twenty buoys and sea marks and four lifesaving stations in this area alone?

Chapter 8

LIGHTHOUSES AND KEEPER HOUSES, 1835–1937

As Cape Ann's fishing industry grew and the granite quarry industry was initiated in the 1820s, the need for navigational aids became apparent. The granite companies shipped their product by water to cities along the eastern and southern coasts. It was noted by government officials that seventy thousand vessels passed by Sandy Bay annually. Fishermen heading to and from the Grand Banks from Gloucester, as well as commercial traders in coastal vessels, were numerous. Shipwrecks were a constant occurrence because of the reefs, shoals and ledges, many of which had not yet been charted or marked. Knowledge of these hazards was known mainly by the local fishermen, but not generally known by the many foreign coasters that plied the waters from Canada down to the West Indies. These coasters carried all sorts of goods, from lumber to bricks, granite, wheat, sand and fish.

Cape Ann already had a few lighthouses. Thacher Island's twin lights were built in 1771 after John Hancock petitioned the Massachusetts Bay Colony General Court for a lighthouse to mark the Londoner Reef near Thacher. Hancock had numerous shipping interests and wanted them protected. In 1801, Annisquam Light was built at the head of the Annisquam River leading into Ipswich Bay. The lighthouses at Eastern Point and Ten Pound Island would not be built until 1832 and 1821, respectively. Straitsmouth Island was ideally suited, located as it is four hundred feet offshore near Gap Head (Straitsmouth Head) at the bay's southeastern end, for a lighthouse to guide vessels toward Rockport Harbor and Pigeon Cove and safely past the treacherous rocks of Avery's Ledge, the Salvages northeast of Straitsmouth and the narrow passage past Thacher to the south.

Straitsmouth Light Station was typical of the small harbor stations. It included the bare minimum of operating infrastructure. Namely, these smaller one-keeper family stations consisted of a lighthouse tower, a keeper's dwelling, an oil house to store fuel oil for the lights and a storage barn or shed. An outhouse was also required, as most keeper dwellings did not have indoor plumbing. In addition, a boat launch ramp or dock was part of the necessary equipment, along with a dory or skiff for transportation to the mainland for supplies, mail and emergencies.

THE FIRST OF THREE LIGHTHOUSES, 1835

The first Straitsmouth light was built in 1835, spurred on by the increasing number of ships sailing to Pigeon Cove for cargoes of granite from Rockport's burgeoning granite industry. Congress appropriated $5,000 for the first lighthouse on June 30, 1834.

Winslow Lewis, the government lighthouse contractor, agreed to build both the tower and the keeper dwelling. The contract read in part:

> *Winslow Lewis on his part agrees and engages to build a Lighthouse and dwelling, House on Straitsmouth Island, Cape Ann, of the following materials, dimensions and descriptions. The light house to be built of hard bricks, form round: Foundation to be laid as deep as necessary to render the fabric secure. The diameter of the base to be seventeen feet, walls three feet thick at the base, uniformly graduated to two feet at the top, where the diameter of the tower is to be nine feet six inches. The height of the tower from the surface of the grounds to be eighteen feet, to have two windows in the tower twelve lights eight by ten glass each. The floor of the tower to be paved with hard brick. On top of the tower to have an arch turned, through which to have a scuttle to have a scuttle to enter the lantern 24 by 15 inches. On the arch to be laid a soapstone deck, eleven feet diameter, four inches thick, in which to have a scuttle 24 by 15. Scuttle door and rabbets covered with copper. Circular stairs connected with a center post to lead from the floor of the tower to within six feet of the deck. Stairs to be made of two-inch planks, planned,*

The first lighthouse built in 1835, with its "Bird Cage" lantern room. *USCGHO.*

eight inches rise an iron ladder, steps two and a half inches wide, ½ inch thick, to lead from the top of the stairs to the scuttle of the lantern. The foundation and walls of the tower to be laid in good lime mortar the outside walls of the tower to be well plastered with Roman Cement and whitewashed twice over, a door six feet by three made of double inch board, crop nailed with strong hinges latch and good locks, post, cap and stool to be dressed stone ten inches square. On the top of the tower to be an iron lantern of an octagon form, the posts to be one and a half inches square to go into the walls of the tower four feet. The height and diameter of the lantern to be enough to admit eighteen lights twelve by nine glass in each octagon. The lower tier to be fitted with copper, the rabbets of the sashes to be three quarters of an inch deep and glazed with the best double glass from the Boston Manufactory. In one of the octagons to be an iron framed door covered with copper four feet by two to sheets tight into the rabbets, with two strong turned buttons. The top of the dome to be formed

> *by sixteen iron rafters concentrating in an iron hoop, four inches wide and nine inches in diameter, covered with copper, thirty ounces to the square foot which is to come down and rivet on the piece that forms the top of the sash, which is to be three inches wide. On the dome, to be a traversing ventilator two and a half feet long and fifteen inches in diameter on which is to be secured a copper vane, three feet long and twenty inches wide, around the lantern to be an iron railing, the posts of which to be one and a quarter inches square, the upper one to be four feet from the deck. The lantern and woodwork of the tower to be painted twice over with white lead except the dome which is to be black. The Light House to have one complete electrical conductor made of copper three quarters of an inch in diameter with points and rabbets…to fit up said Light House with six patent lamps and six fourteen-inch reflectors, to have six ounces pure silver in each reflector, tin butts for keeping the oil, and all the necessary apparatus in the same manner as the Light Houses have been fitted up by Mr. Winslow Lewis.*

The first lighthouse was only nineteen feet tall and poorly constructed, leaky and with lamps out of plumb. Not only that, but it was situated five hundred feet too far away from the point of the island it was intended to warn against. The lighthouse establishment's engineer, I.W.P Lewis (Winslow Lewis's nephew), visited in 1842 and described the tower as "laid up in bad lime mortar," its woodwork rotten and whole structure very leaky. The dwelling was also poorly built.

There were six lamps in use when Lewis visited, each equipped with a thirteen-and-a-half-inch reflector. Four of the lamps were "out of plum," and one of them faced the door to the lantern and had thus "burned for six years without the possibility of being seen." In addition to the poor construction, Lewis pointed out that the lighthouse, on the island central eastern shore, was built in the wrong place. His report stated:

> *The uses of this light as originally designed, apart from its local services as a harbor beacon, was to enable vessels to run through the narrow channel between thatcher's island and the salvages which purpose was completely frustrated by the contractor setting the tower about 500 feet West of the only position where it could serve as a mark to clear Alden's ledge* [Avery's Ledge] *and the flat grounds to the eastward.*
>
> *The present light is a positive injury to navigation, as it misleads strangers, who frequently get ashore on the low eastern part of the island,*

or strike on Alden's ledge, upon which there is no buoy or other mark. The tower is not worth repainting, and should be taken down, and a firm and substantial structure erected on the eastern point of the island. One lamp only is required for this locality instead of the six now used.

Another inspection in 1843 by the local superintendent called the lighthouse (only eight years old) "[a] miserable old brick tower"; the report called keeper Davis "an excellent and attentive man and careful of everything." The superintendent added that access to the station was difficult in high seas, and he recommended the addition of boat ways (a boat landing ramp). A boathouse and landing ramp were built in 1867 at the western end of the island at the Gap and remained there until 1936, when the USCG abandoned the island. Keeper Davis reported how leaky the tower was—it had a half-inch coating of ice inside in January—and suggested that a new tower was needed.

Several vessels were lost during storms in the 1830s and 1840s in the vicinity of Straitsmouth Island. Local navigation was improved somewhat by the addition of a buoy near Avery's Rock, north of the island, in 1845. A much-needed lifesaving station was established opposite the island on the mainland in 1874.

THE 1851 LIGHTHOUSE

In 1851, construction began on a new lighthouse, a twenty-four-foot-tall stone tower eighty-seven yards closer to the island's northeast point. This lighthouse had a unique octagonal shape with a "Bird Cage" lantern. A fixed sixth-order Fresnel lens was added in 1857 that was eventually changed to a six-second white blinking light beacon. A triangular skeletal tower structure was built to hang the temporary light while the old lighthouse was dismantled and a new one constructed.

Edwin Adams was contracted to rebuild the tower and a new lantern, dated December 30, 1850. (Adams also built the Thacher towers later in 1861.) The bid price was $1,948. The contract reads:

Tower to be built would be octagonal, height from surface of ground 26 feet, diameter of base at angles 16 feet, that of the top 9 feet, the foundation laid on solid ledge exterior walls [base] *of granite. Walls to be three feet*

The second lighthouse built in 1851 was relocated much closer to the end of the island. This 1915 postcard shows the skeletal tower. *Robert Ambrogi Collection.*

thick at base graduated to two feet at the top. Stone not less than 10 inches thick or more than 12 inches. Circular stone stairs from floor to within 6 feet of the lantern where there is to be a stone platform four inches thick forming one fourth of a circle. Stairs to be 9 inches rise and 12 inches tread one end to go four inches into the wall the other to form one continued newel in the center of the tower. An iron ladder 6-feet, two windows 12 lights each, 8 by 10 glazed with thick glass. Door to be made of sheet iron, one eighth of an inch thick. Lantern is to be wrought iron large enough to fit 6 lights 24 by 15 inch each octagon and two 12 by 15-inch lights.

LAST LIGHTHOUSE, 1896

By 1896, the light again needed rebuilding, and the current lighthouse was built. This copy of the notice to mariners announced the new light and its new location, dated July 21, 1896: "Notice is hereby given that on or about July 30, 1896, the 6th order fixed white light at this station, on the NE point of Straitsmouth, N. side of Cape Ann will be moved to be exhibited from the new tower recently erected 45 feet N+W from the present temporary tower."

A panoramic photograph of both Straitsmouth and Thacher Islands dated around the turn of the century. *SBHS*.

The bid was approved on January 21, 1896, to build a new tower for $2,984.60, plus materials at $442.52. The thirty-seven-foot cylindrical brick tower was erected on the center of the original foundation of the 1851 lighthouse and still stands on Straitsmouth today.

A boat slip and 315-foot wooden walkway were added in 1867 and rebuilt in 1894, enabling the keepers to more easily negotiate walking directly from the keeper house to the tower to tend the lights and clean the lenses.

The U.S. Lighthouse Service ordered that all lighthouses must store their kerosene fuel (mineral oil) for the lights in brick buildings with slate roofs to guard against fires with the highly combustible fuel material. The brick and slate oil house was added about 1905.

Some 120 running feet of stone and gravel walk was laid, the boathouse was moved and secured on stone piers and minor repairs were made to the fuel house and footbridge leading to the tower at Gap Cove west end in 1900.

A letter dated August 15, 1901, from Lieutenant Colonel of Engineers W.S. Stanton to the Light-House Board requested a derrick and a landing near the station for ready landing of supplies for $493, to re-shingle the dwelling for $202 and to provide a sink drain for $40. This was because "the light-station boat-slip is a long distance from the dwelling," about one-third of a mile from the keeper house.

On June 12, 1903, a letter from keeper Thomas Newcomb to the second lighthouse district inspector indicated that he had burned down the dwelling house and "only the brick walls now remain." See the ninth chapter for details on this story.

THE KEEPER'S DWELLINGS

Two keeper houses have been built here. The first, in 1835, was of brick, built in conjunction with the construction of the first lighthouse. Not much is known about this house, although it was situated behind the second wood-frame Victorian-styled keeper house, built in 1878.

The contract between Winslow Lewis, the government contractor, and David Henshaw, the collector of the District of Boston and Charlestown, on behalf of the United States of America, is dated June 17, 1835, and reads as follows:

> *The dwelling house to be of brick thirty four feet by twenty feet, walls to be twelve inches thick, one story, of eight feet high, divided into two rooms with an entry between the stairs to be in the entry, to go into the chambers which are to be lathed and plastered. Chimney in each end of the house, fire place in each room, iron mantel pieces, closet back of the stairs in the entry with doors opening into each parlour, door under the stairs to open to the steps leading into the cellar, which is to be under the whole house six feet deep, walls of stone not less than twenty inches thick well painted and whitewashed. Roof rectangular covered with good dry merchantable boards, shingled with good shingles laid not more the four- and one-half inches to the weather. Three windows in each room sixteen lights 8 by 10 each one window in each chamber 12 lights 8 by 10 all floors to be laid double, all the doors to be four paneled except the front door which is to have frieze panels, good hinges and latches & good lock on the front door. The inside walls and ceiling to be lathed and plastered and the inside work to be finished in plain decent style and with good seasoned timber. Also a porch or kitchen attached to the dwelling house fourteen by twelve feet in the clear,*

A rare photo of both keeper houses, the 1835 (*center*) and the 1878 (*far left*). The small barn on the right burned down in 1903. *USCGHO.*

> *walls twelve inches thick, eight feet high the room to be lathed and plastered with double floors, two windows and one door, crane trammels and hooks in the fireplace in the porch or kitchen, one side of the chimney or sink with a spout leading through the stone walls.*
>
> *All the woodwork inside and out to be painted with two coats of good paints gutters to lead round the house, with spouts to convey off the water, an outhouse of brick, five feet by four, the roof shingle door painted. The whole to be completed in a workman like manner by the first day of September next.*

The overall cost of both the lighthouse and the dwelling was $3,300.

NEW KEEPER DWELLING, 1878

A one-and-a-half-story wood-frame keeper's house was erected in 1878 in front of the existing dwelling, similar in design to the keeper house on Thacher and using the same plans. It was a two-story Victorian with three bedrooms, a dining room, a kitchen and a parlor.

The island provided space for the keepers to grow vegetables and graze cows and sheep, as well as keep chickens; goats were used to keep the

The 1878 keeper house about 1925. *USCGHO.*

vegetation down. Keepers cleared the fields and built stone walls to enclose the farm animals and provide areas to grow crops of corn, tomatoes, potatoes, beans and beets. Aerial photos from the 1950s clearly show where these stone walls were built. A milking barn once existed behind the original keeper dwelling.

The island was manned by a single family most of the time; keepers were present from 1835 until 1936. Upkeep and maintenance were a regular part of the daily chores. Storms out of the northeast regularly ravaged the island, as it had no natural barrier to the winds coming across Sandy Bay. Reviewing the annual reports from the lighthouse service indicated repairs and replacements, as well as painting and annual appropriations for needed essentials. Here is a sampling of various notes from the *Light-House Board Annual Reports*:

- 1877: New keeper dwelling is under construction.
- 1878: One-and-a-half-story keeper's frame dwelling is erected.
- 1879: Boat slip is rebuilt, exterior walls of keeper dwelling and woodshed are repainted.
- 1881: The dwelling house woodwork is overhauled and repainted, and the chimney is provided with a cap for its better draft.
- 1881: Boat slip is repaired and refastened, dwelling interior is painted and house pump is repaired.
- 1885: New windows in tower.

- 1886: New windows in tower, re-shingled roof old dwelling, repairs to lantern and boat slip.
- 1893: The foot bridge from the dwelling to the tower is rebuilt, the boat slip is repaired and minor repairs are made to the tower and dwelling.
- 1896: The tower and workroom are rebuilt on the same foundations. Minor repairs are made.
- 1896: Moved 45' S¾E to temporary tower May 11, 1896.
- 1897: Moved tower 45' N¾W.
- 1900: Some 120 running feet of stone and gravel walk are laid, the boathouse is moved and secured on stone piers and minor repairs are made to the fuel house and footbridge leading to the tower.
- 1902: A derrick on the north side of the island, to facilitate the landing of supplies, and a platform around it are built. Various repairs are made.
- 1903: Twenty feet of outer end of boat slip are renewed.
- 1905: Oil house is built, and boat slip, barn and walkway are repaired.

Straitsmouth was no longer listed in the annual reports after 1912. Reports ceased in 1917, when the Coast Guard was established the prior year. In addition to the basic structures on the island—the lighthouse, keeper dwelling and barn—there were others added between 1867 and 1905, as noted in the list of annual reports of 1867: a boat slip and a 315-foot walkway or footbridge from the keeper house to the lighthouse.

The boat slip consisted of a wooden ramp about seventy-five feet long at the far western end of the island at the Gap. Later, a boathouse was added to store the keeper's small rowboats. The boathouse was moved farther down the bluff and set on stone piers to get closer to the water. The boat slip was repaired many times between 1879 and 1896. This structure lasted until 1937, when it was taken down after the keepers were moved off the island and the station closed.

A footbridge walkway was built in about 1867 from the keeper dwelling to the lighthouse to facilitate the keeper's ability to enter the lighthouse door, which was ten feet above the rocky ledge. This footbridge was rebuilt in 1893, and a new one was built in 1896 in conjunction with the construction of the new tower.

A derrick was built on the northeast side near the keeper dwelling beside a small inlet that was navigable by small craft at high tide. A letter dated

Above: The old boathouse and boat ramp, with visitors, about 1925; it was located in the same location as the new 2019 boat ramp. *Randy Saville.*

Left: The original footbridge leading from the keeper house to the lighthouse has been rebuilt three times since 1867. This photo was taken in 1925. *USCGHO.*

August 15, 1901, from Lieutenant Colonel of Engineers W.S. Stanton to the Light-House Board requested a derrick and a platform around it to be built to make a landing near the station for ready landing of supplies for $493, as "the light-station boat-slip is a long distance from the dwelling."

A general order went out from the Light-House Board to all light stations to construct brick-and-slate fireproof oil houses to store the flammable kerosene now used for lighthouse lamps. Mineral oil, or kerosene as it came to be more commonly termed, was one of those many petroleum products, and its abundance and consequent low cost, compared to the scarcer and

The derrick was located closer to the house on the north-facing ledge in 1901. *SBHS.*

more costly oils used earlier, soon made it the fuel of choice for the far-flung stations of the lighthouse establishment. When it was first introduced, its much greater flammability and ease of ignition, compared with the earlier whale/lard/colza oils that had long been in use, made it a substance greatly respected, if not outright feared. It has been described as "volatile, inflammable, and explosive." This simple fact is the very reason that separate fireproof oil houses were mandated. Storing the lamp fuel in the light towers or in the typically adjacent workrooms, as was commonly done, was no longer a safe practice. As early as 1855, scientists of the fledgling Light-House Board—always on the search for brighter, more efficient and more economical lamp fuels—had been experimenting with various petroleum products. It was not until 1877, however, that the first use of kerosene as a lighthouse fuel was reported (see "Chronology of Aids to Navigation, 1716–1939" by Coast Guard historian Truman Strobridge). The first use of kerosene within a first-order Fresnel lens was at Navesink, New Jersey, in 1883; by 1885, it had become the principal illuminant in use at stations across the United States.

Exactly when the Light-House Board directed the construction of separate fireproof oil houses at each station is unclear. An 1884 letter from John Newton, then the chairman of the board's Committee on Engineering, to Admiral Stephen Rowan, the board chairman, reported that the committee

All light stations were required to have a brick-and-slate fireproof oil house to store the highly flammable kerosene lamp oil. This one was built in 1905. *Author's collection.*

had approved a standard plan for a brick oil house. The annual report of the board for 1887 stated, "In view of the danger which necessarily follows upon the use of mineral oil as an illuminant, it is thought that an isolated fireproof structure for the storing of its supplies of oil should be provided at all light stations." The Straitsmouth oil house was built in 1905, approximately ten by fifteen feet of brick with slate roofing tiles.

North Atlantic Fleet Comes to Rockport in View of Straitsmouth

In the late 1880s, the North Atlantic Fleet made frequent annual visits to Rockport each summer and anchored directly off Straitsmouth with its giant battleships and cruisers. The fleet often held sea trials of its newest ship, racing the thirty miles from Straitsmouth north to Cape Porpoise in Maine and back to test speeds and endurance of the latest naval battle wagons. The fleet conducted maneuvers around Straitsmouth and Thacher using some thirty naval craft, including battleships, destroyers, submarines, cruisers and support craft. Many ships of the Great White Fleet appeared in Sandy Bay in summers before and after their around-the-world cruise in 1907, returning in 1909.

The most exciting and interesting arrival of the U.S. Navy occurred in 1906, led by Rear Admiral Robley "Fighting Bob" Evans aboard his flagship USS *Maine*. He brought two divisions of the Atlantic fleet, which included the USS *Alabama*, USS *Kearsarge*, USS *Iowa*, USS *Missouri*, USS *Illinois*, USS *Indiana*, USS *Kentucky* and the gunboat *Yankton*. Admiral Evans was a very high-profile naval officer. His visit brought the most battleships ever to Sandy Bay. He arrived in June and did not leave until August. He and his crews were entertained and given the run of the town, and special arrangements were made for crew members at the town hall. The crews accounted for more than five thousand men, which equaled the population of Rockport at the time. Several family members of the crew were put up at local hotels, including in the Turks Head Inn near Loblolly Cove and the Ocean View House in Pigeon Cove. Banquet dinners and receptions were held all over town. Baseball games at the South End, Winter's Field and Webster's Field, as well as on Straitsmouth and Thacher Islands, were played by town teams against teams from the ships. Each night, the ships put on spectacular searchlight exhibitions, and each ship's band played regularly on board, as well as at the various hotels. Some ten thousand people came

The North Atlantic Fleet lay at anchor in 1906 adjacent to Straitsmouth in the background to the right. *SBHS.*

for the searchlight displays. On July 20, 1906, a total of thirty-five vessels was anchored in Sandy Bay in view of the keepers on Straitsmouth. The *Boston Globe* reported that "the fleet was one of the most formidable naval forces ever assembled under the American flag."

THE LIGHT

This note appeared in the *Lighthouse Service Annual Report* for 1930:

> *Superintendent of Lighthouses suggests that they replace the 6th order fixed lens* [oil lamp equipment] *with a 4th order fixed lens having a 35mm Type A incandescent oil vapor lamp showing a fixed green light. Est. cost $1200. Will increase light from 140 to 800 candlepower. With the addition of a Gas Buoy at Salvages will compensate for discontinuance of one of the twin lights at Thacher. In August the 4th order lens was replaced by a 5th order fixed with a green shade.*

These were all Fresnel lenses made of crystal glass prisms that concentrated and focused 85 percent of a lamp's light, versus the 20 percent focused with the parabolic reflectors of the time. Its design enabled construction of lenses of large size and short focal length without the weight and volume of material in conventional lens designs. Fresnel lighthouse lenses are ranked by "order," a measure of refracting power, with a first order the largest, most powerful and expensive and a sixth order the smallest. The order is based on the focal length of the lens. A first-order lens has the longest focal length (used in both lighthouses on Thacher Island; the original 1861 south tower Fresnel lens is on display at the Cape Ann Museum), while the sixth has the shortest.

Coastal lighthouses generally use first-, second- or third-order lenses, while harbor lights and beacons use fourth-, fifth- or sixth-order lenses, such as the one at Straitsmouth. The lighthouse on Straitsmouth had a sixth-order lens in 1857, then a fourth order in June 1895 and a fifth order in 1930. On April 11, 1933, another change was made from fifth-order lens to a 300mm lens, as well as to electrify with incandescent bulbs and automated the light. An electric cable from the mainland near the Gap was laid across island and connected to a 220-110 step-down transformer and automatic time switch, which essentially automated the light, requiring no human

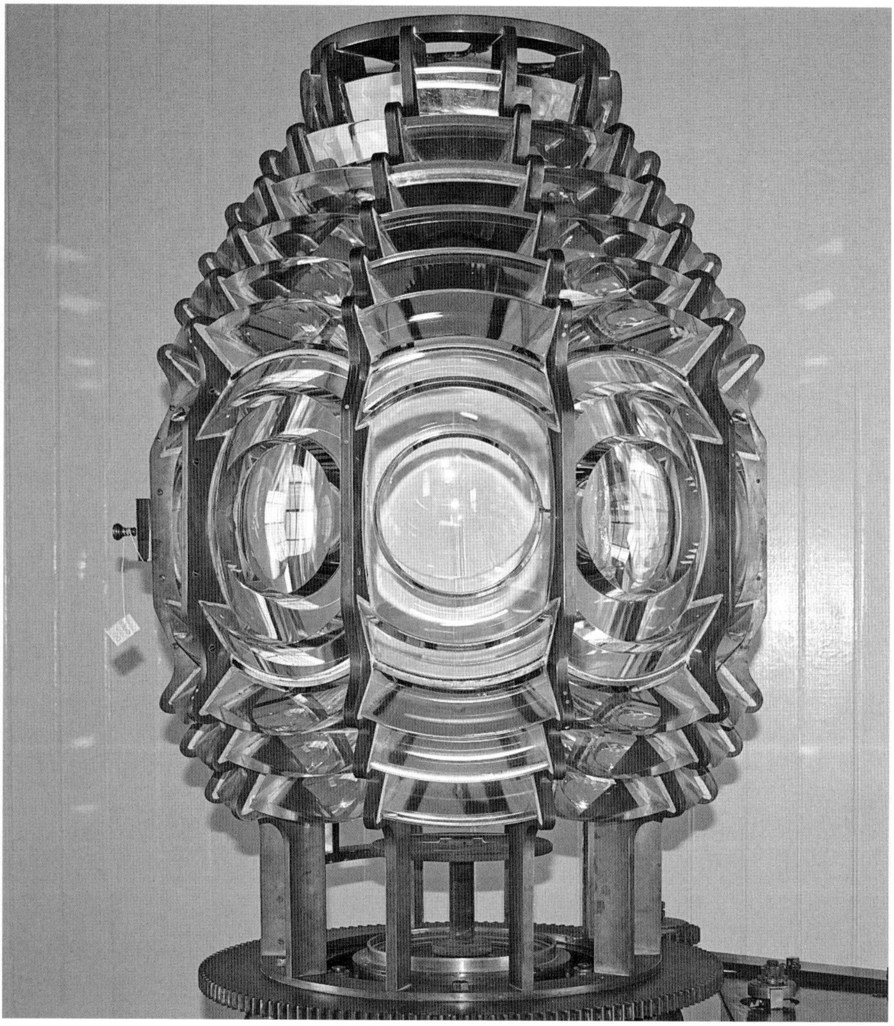

Above: A fifth-order Fresnel lens with a green flashing light replaced the fourth-order lens in 1930. *Author's collection.*

Opposite, top: The lighthouse was severely damaged, losing its entry cabin, during the 1991 "Perfect Storm." *Author's collection.*

Opposite, bottom: The current solar-powered LED light still features a flashing green beacon. *Author's collection.*

interaction. On October 18, the commissioner proposed discontinuation of the keeper position and declared as surplus the dwelling, boat slip, oil house, wooden outhouse and wooden walkway, estimating the sale value of land to be $1,000 and buildings $1,000.

In 1991, the "Perfect Storm," sometimes referred to as the "No-Name Storm," destroyed the old entryway cabin to the tower.

During the one hundred years that the light station was active (1835–1936), it saw three wars: the Civil War, the Spanish-American War and World War I. It served during twenty-six presidencies, including those of Andrew Jackson, Abraham Lincoln, Theodore Roosevelt, Woodrow Wilson and, finally, Franklin Delano Roosevelt.

In 1839, just four years after the first lighthouse was built on Straitsmouth, only 156 lighthouses existed in sixteen eastern states of the new nation. By 1935, the number had quadrupled from coast to coast. Lighthouse illumination went from sperm oil (whale oil) to kerosene, mineral oil, oil vapor and electric lights—today, the light and foghorn are solar powered. We moved from old technology like argand oil lamps to Fresnel lenses to large electric aero beacons that can be seen twenty-two miles out to sea. Today, it has an LED single-row light that can be seen up to eight miles away with a blinking green light.

Chapter 9

THE LIGHT KEEPERS, 1835–1933

Naturally, light stations needed the day-to-day management of a human hand. Keepers were essential to the proper operation and maintenance of these sentinels of the sea. Straitsmouth Station had a relatively short existence of just about one hundred years. Thacher Island had lighthouse keepers in attendance for two hundred years (1771–1939), when the U.S. Coast Guard took over and continued to man the island until 1980.

Lighthouse keepers were generally blue-collar folks, men mostly from seafaring or military backgrounds. Annual salaries were low, between $250 and $600 per year in the years between 1835 through 1925. Many keepers were appointed through political patronage and often lost their position upon a change in party or local representative.

Wives sometimes replaced their husbands upon their death, although that did not happen on Straitsmouth. The keeper and his wife were partners in the operation of the station, and each had a variety of skills. They had to be boat handlers, farmers, carpenters, stonemasons, plumbers, animal handlers, accountants, record keepers, mechanics, painters and engineers. Daily chores included climbing the lighthouse to clean the lens and lantern room glass, trim the wicks and fill the lamps with oil. Keeper dwellings, light towers and maintenance barns were to be kept spotless because inspectors could arrive unannounced on a quarterly basis for "white glove inspections."

Every keeper was required to keep a daily logbook. Unfortunately, most of the Straitsmouth logs from the National Archives files were lost in a major fire in the 1920s. I have reviewed most of the later logs on Thacher, which I found to be not very illuminating. They were basically used to record the weather, minor personnel changes and issues, keepers leaving the island to go to town and returning, number of hours the foghorn operated, or amount of coal or lamp oil used. Very seldom did we see expansive or detailed reports on lifesaving efforts or shipwrecks.

In 1915, the U.S. Coast Guard was formed by the merger of the U.S. Life-Saving Service with the U.S. Revenue Marine Cutter Service. In 1929, rumors began that the island would be "unattended," meaning that the crew would be relieved of duty and transferred. Internal memos between the office of the superintendent of lighthouses and the Department of Commerce Commissioner of Lighthouses seemed ominous. One memo, dated June 26, 1929, noted, "The old barn and small shed at Straitsmouth Light Station and the old barn at Annisquam Light Station are in need of extensive repairs, as they are of no further use to the Government, Bureaus authority is requested to tear down these out-buildings." Notes scribbled on this memo indicate that this was the first step in decommissioning the station.

In 1931, the lighthouse service conducted a complete inventory of the Straitsmouth Light Station on May 12. This was usually the first step in selling a government property. A recommendation on aids to navigation was sent on April 11, 1933: "Change order [meaning the size of the Fresnel lens] and illuminant of above light and make same unattended." Under the heading "Necessity," it was noted, "To reduce operating expenses on account of limited funds appropriated for maintenance purposes."

The description of the work noted, "It is proposed to lay a cable to and across the island, connect a 220-110 step-down transformer and install a 300m.m. lantern…when this has been accomplished authority is likewise requested to discontinue the present keeper's position and close the buildings on reservation…this action an approximate savings of $1320 under salaries, Keepers of Lighthouse and a minimum of $125 under general expenses."

Another memo, from October 18, 1933, to the secretary of commerce from Superintendent Chief Clerk was titled "Proposed discontinuance, position keeper, Straitsmouth Light Station." It went on to say, "The Bureau is advised that the light at above station has been changed to unattended, making the services of a keeper at the station no longer necessary, and the Keeper, Hoyt P. Smith has been transferred to position Keeper (3rd Asst.) at Ashtabula Light Station, Ohio."

Coming out of the Depression in 1929, the government was making a major cost-cutting effort. In July 1930, President Franklin D. Roosevelt ordered the lighthouse commissioner to discontinue the north tower light on Thacher, much to the chagrin and outrage of the fishermen, town officials and residents of Cape Ann. His reason: "Cost cutting and the depression." It took the government two years to effect the change because it was in the process of changing over from oil lamps to electricity.

Finally, in an April 26, 1937 letter to the director of procurement in the Treasury Department from the chief of the Division of the Bureau of Lighthouses, the first paragraph said it all: "You are advised that the following portion of the Lighthouse Reservation at Straitsmouth Island, off Rockport, Massachusetts, indicated as Parcel No. 2 on the attached blueprint of Drawing No. 2314, is surplus to the needs of this Department." And it went on for three more pages about the location, value and the possibility of renting or selling the property.

In 1939, the U.S. Lighthouse Service was absorbed into the newly formed U.S. Coast Guard. It was at this juncture that serious talk began about closing Straitsmouth. Official word came in 1939 that the station was to be closed. The USCG personnel would move across the cove to be billeted at the Gap Cove Life-Saving Station just a few hundred yards southwest of the island. The lighthouse was to be maintained as an active aid to navigation and was to be managed by the Coast Guard crew from Straitsmouth Life-Saving Station.

The last keeper was Hoyt Smith, who was transferred to the Ashtabula, Ohio Light Station on October 10, 1933. After his stint in Ohio, he was assigned to Boon Island, Maine, on July 8, 1935, as second assistant—one of the most barren and lonely stations in the nation. He finally left and ended his career as a U.S. Coast Guard boatswain's mate on June 21, 1941. Although the station was not immediately sold, it was rented twice. That story continues in the tenth chapter.

During the 100 years that the island had keepers attending the lights, all sixteen keepers had interesting and sometimes tragic stories of their own. Some had made important contributions to the lighthouse service, others displayed great courage in saving mariners from sinking ships and others had varied backgrounds not only as lighthouse keepers but also as quarrymen, businessmen and community leaders. Keepers generally served from a few months up to 20 years from the longest-serving keeper, Thomas W. Newcomb. A few served on many other light stations, while a few only served on Straitsmouth and never continued in another lighthouse. Many led sad lives; they lost children to disease or died of consumption or heart disease or cancer, and many lost their first or second wives. Two died while in service on the island, most resigned and three were transferred. A few were "removed," which could mean anything from "fired for cause" to a new political regime that had to make room for a political appointee. Most keepers served between the ages of thirty-seven and fifty-five. Nehemiah Knowlton served a 14-year term froms age sixty-one to seventy-four. The sixteen keepers had twenty-one wives and forty-one children, of whom ten died at an early age. Only two keepers were unmarried. Many of the keepers served in the army or navy or in lifesaving services. Many served in the various wars during the 140-year span from the Revolutionary War to the War of 1812, the Civil War, the Spanish-American War and World War I. Eight of them lived well into their seventies and beyond.

I have chosen to write about those who I felt had the most fascinating backgrounds.

BENJAMIN WILLIAMS ANDREWS, 1786–1840

We begin with the first Straitsmouth Light Station keeper, Benjamin Andrews, in September 1835. He died in service on the island on August 5, 1840. His death record lists him as a tailor. We recently found his gravestone in the Old Parish Burying Ground in Rockport.

We know very little of his life during his forty-five years from 1786 until 1835, before he began working on Straitsmouth. Was he a soldier during the French and Indian Wars or during the War of 1812, when he would have been twenty-six? We know he was one of three children.

Andrews was born on February 9, 1786, in Gloucester's Sandy Bay Parish and married Mary Soper (Polly) Marshall in March 1806. He went to Straitsmouth at age forty-nine with Polly, who was forty-eight. They had four children: Mary Williams Andrews (1806), Benjamin Williams Andrews (no. 2) (1813), Betsey Foster Andrews (1813) and Sophia Oakes Andrews (1817). Sophia died at one year and six months old. Mary and Betsey lived with their mother and remained single their entire lives. Mary was a seamstress/tailoress, and Betsey was the proprietor of a variety store. They died at seventy-eight and seventy-five, respectively. Benjamin (no.

2) was a fisherman or mariner and was listed as a butcher on his death record, having died of consumption at age seventy-eight in 1887. He is buried at Union Cemetery in Rockport.

There are mysteries. Why did a tailor work as a light keeper on Straitsmouth Island? What did he die of? He lost his mother when he was as young as five and got a new mother with a baby sister bearing his mother's name when he was twelve. He lost an eighteen-month-old child. There's something about the way his two daughters never left home, how they cared for their mother until her death at the age of eighty-two, that seems part of an alcoholic family's story—his death, at the age of fifty-four, was described as "jaundice."

Benjamin Sr.'s death certificate said he died on Straitsmouth of "jaundice," which is a symptom, not a disease. The most common causes of jaundice include liver infection, pancreatic cancer, bile duct obstruction, hepatitis or cirrhosis with or without alcoholism as a precursor. We will never know.

Benjamin Andrews was awarded a medal for heroism by the Massachusetts Humane Society for his rescue of two men who were washed overboard and clinging to the mast of their sailboat in March 1839.

The Humane Society of the Commonwealth of Massachusetts medal for bravery, awarded to keeper Benjamin Andrews in 1839. *SBHS.*

The medal reads:

> *The Humane Society of the Commonwealth of Massachusetts to Capt. Benj. W. Andrews* [front]
>
> *In testimony of their approbation of his exertions whereby the lives of two men were preserved when in imminent danger of drowning near Sandy Bay on the 16th March 1839.* [reverse]

The story in the Gloucester newspaper read:

> *Fortunate Rescue and Praiseworthy Conduct. Mister Andrews, the keeper of the Straitsmouth Island Light, off Cape Ann, accidentally saw two men clinging to the masts of an upset sailboat, floating by the Island out to sea. He lost no time and pushing off his wherry end pulling alone to their assistance. He reached them with considerable difficulty and danger, as the sea was very rough and the wind strong. He however succeeded in getting them into his boat senseless, and unable to help themselves, but not without periling his own life by the sinking of his boat, the waves rolling into her while he struggled to get the men out of the water. He reached the shore, however, almost exhausted, and by the laudable exertions of his wife and daughter, the only persons on the island, the half-drowned men were got on shore. A signal of distress was made, and in about an hour assistance was had from Sandy Bay. In the meantime, every effort was made to bring these men to their senses. They were finally resuscitated and are now doing well. They belonged to Sandy Bay. Mr. and Mrs. Andrews and daughter, throughout the painful scene, showed remarkable energy, firmness, and presence of mind, truly worthy of public gratitude and reward. The sufferers owe their lives to the distinguished heroism of the three persons on the island, towards whom they will feel everlasting gratitude an obligation.*

CAPTAIN JOHN DAVIS, 1784–1852

Captain John Davis was born on February 7, 1784, the son of Daniel Davis and Lydia (Riggs), who married on August 2, 1774. They had eight children, three girls and five boys. Captain Davis was married twice, first to Esther Willson on December 1, 1805. She died on November 5, 1843, at age fifty-five.

He wasted little time and at age sixty remarried Margaret Weaver, the widow of William Butman, on April 29, 1844, when she was fifty-nine. Davis is listed in the Rockport Directory as mariner and teacher. He had a brother, Captain Timothy Riggs Davis, born on November 28, 1781, who died on February 2, 1848, at age sixty-six. He was also listed as a mariner. Captain Davis was in the navy, but we are unsure of the dates. He had a second brother, named Daniel, born on April 16, 1780, all of which was noted on his death record. Captain Davis died on July 7, 1852, at age sixty-eight.

Captain John Davis was related to the original 1699 grantee owner of Straitsmouth Island, Captain James Davis (1635–1715). Based on the dates, John could have been a grandson of James or a great-grandson. Much of the information found about Captain Davis was in the U.S. Lighthouse Establishment letter books at the National Archives. They give an interesting picture of Davis's eight-year term on the island.

John Davis was appointed keeper on July 15, 1841, having been recommended by the Honorable Leverett Saltonstall, House of Representatives. His appointment was delayed because it was thought the letter of appointment had been incorrectly sent to the current keeper on July 1 as opposed to Superintendent of Lights (Boston District) Levi Lincoln, Esq., who would have forwarded it directly to Davis. This was a prime example of the political patronage that many keepers were entangled in and how poorly managed the lighthouse establishment was in 1840.

On September 6, 1841, Fifth Auditor of the Treasury Department Stephen Pleasanton (in charge of all lighthouses in the nation), told Superintendent of Lights Levi Lincoln that he had received a letter from the keeper about the poor condition of the lighthouse and told him to advertise in the spring in one newspaper twice a week for a fortnight for proposals to take down and rebuild the lighthouse. He also said that the keeper recommended the tower be built eighty-seven yards from the old one. He cautioned that if done "vessels might be deceived as to the identity of the light and be run ashore and be lost." This is when we learn that the first lighthouse was built too far from the eastern point of the island to be effective.

On April 6, 1842, Davis wrote about using a stove or burning wood in the tower to keep the oil warm versus using the "nurse lamp." (He alluded to Keeper Darling at Marblehead Light, who had successes with this type of lamp.) He also mentioned that Charles Wheeler's new lamp for warming oil used only sixteen to twenty dollars' worth of fuel for the winter. Charles Wheeler was a keeper on Thacher from 1836 until 1849. Wheeler patented a device to prevent oil from freezing in the lamp. He once wrote to the lighthouse superintendent, "I have invented and put to use, a good and useful lighthouse lamp, which saves the government not less than $30 per year. They have now been in use eleven years which has made a saving, in stoves and fuel, of not less than $300."

In a letter book of Fifth Auditor Stephen Pleasanton dated August 9, 1842, and sent to Superintendent of Lights Lincoln, he responded to Lincoln's report on the condition of the lighthouses and the conduct of the keepers within his district. After he had reviewed all the light stations under his purview from Newburyport to Cape Cod, he wrote about Straitsmouth Island Light, "You will cause ways [boat landing ramp] to be made from the boathouse to the water, at an expense not exceeding 65 dollars, as estimated, and will pay the keeper 50.40 dollars for repairs done by him last year, beyond what you then authorized, but which you state to have been necessary." This is the first we hear about a boathouse and a boat ramp (ways) to be built.

He also reported that "Thatcher Island Light will be constructing a landing place for boats, by blasting and removing rock authorizing the spending of $250 to do so." This would occasion the first use of a boat landing ramp on the western side of Thacher. Note the misspelling of Thacher, which occurs often in official government documents for many years.

On January16, 1843, Davis wrote a letter to his superior indicating that the lighthouse leaked very badly. "The inside of the lighthouse is well coated with ice, about half an inch thick" He mentioned that the walls of the tower were three feet thick and that if they were six feet thick and solid, the rain would still penetrate. He went on to suggest rebuilding the tower with a double wall with space between and hoped that it would be rebuilt next summer.

On March 24, 1843, in a letter to the Honorable John C. Spencer (secretary of the treasury) he stated that he has kept this light nearly two years and has used the nurse lamp for the purpose of warming the oil in the lamps during both winters. He has kept a separate account of the oil used in the nurse lamps the past winter "which amounted to one gallon and three gills." He has been able to keep the oil in a perfect liquid state using the nurse lamp.

He stated that the lighthouse only has six lamps, but if there were twelve there would be no adjustment of cost. He recommended that all lighthouses use the nurse lamp.

On April 18, 1843, Pleasanton wrote to Lincoln about the poor tower constructed by Winslow Lewis (Lewis won the contract to build forty lighthouses and keeper dwellings) and insisted that Lewis rebuild the tower in a better location—if he didn't, a new contractor would be found. He also wanted to learn more about the "nurse lamp" and wanted Davis to be told only to use government-approved lamps.

On June 2, 1843, Pleasanton wrote to Lincoln again about approval to shingle the outhouse and to have the keeper (Davis) send him a sample of the nurse lamp; he complained that Davis "has very improperly been writing to the Secretary of the Treasury about it, a thing I have never heard of before."

On August 12, 1843, Davis wrote that when I.W.P. Lewis did the inspection of the tower on September 1, 1842, Davis had signed it without thoroughly reading it. In this letter, he wanted the record to show that he believed the tower to be well built, the lamps did not reflect directly against the door and that the chandelier was set to the best advantage. "The woodwork in the tower is sound no decay. No vessel has ever been wrecked on the island since I have been here. The statement to which my name is affixed in I.W.P. Lewis' report was written by him and presented to me to sign a few minutes before he left the island, consequently I did not give it the attention, that the nature of the case demanded."

On August 19, 1843, in a letter to Winslow Lewis from Louis Dennis, master mason, it's noted that Lewis sent him to inspect the leaky tower and the other structures. He commended Davis for his "improvements to the tower roof, addition of shingles and saddle louvers on the ridge. His work on the barn, boathouse and out-buildings." He mentioned that "the dwelling house is built of brick and of good materials furnished in a plain neat and substantial manner and displays in the extraordinary convenience of its internal arrangement a remarkable degree of judgement, and good taste."

On October 20, 1843, Pleasanton wrote to William. A. Wellman, an engineer, requesting a model of the oil lamp heater from Thacher's, asking to have one built and sent to him. This is Charles Wheeler's patented lamp.

On August 4, 1845, Pleasanton wrote a letter to District Superintendent Marcus Morton, indicating that he had a letter from Davis requesting permission to enclose about two acres of land near the lighthouse for the purpose of cultivation at an expense not to exceed $89.50. He told him to give permission because "[a]s this will contribute to the comfort of the keeper and his family, whose salary is small you will grant permission asked," but Davis was "not allowed" to do the work himself, as it was against the law to make any allowance to the keeper or other officers for extra work. Bureaucracy at its finest.

If one looks at aerial photographs taken in the 1950s, there were many stone walls that crisscross the island. These were built in the 1840s not only for vegetable gardens but also as enclosures to contain sheep, goats, cows and chickens that the keeper families depended on for food beyond a constant diet of fish. There were also barns and a milking barn pictured in the early years.

On November 19, 1845, this notice appeared in the *New York Herald* newspaper: "Schr. *Garner, Jewett,* of Boston, was the schooner reported ashore at Straitsmouth Island, near Gloucester—she parted her chains in the blow the morning of the 10th; crew saved, with sails and rigging—hull would be sold. A sloop belonging to Pigeon Cove, was driven to sea in the same blow, and has not since been heard from." Davis was no doubt involved in saving the crew.

On January 30, 1846, Davis wrote to the Honorable D.P. King, superintendent of lights (Boston):

> *Sir, Last February a Schr. of and from Thomaston, ME laden with lime was totally lost on the flat ground a sunken ledge lying about two miles northeasterly from this island. It was blowing a heavy gale from N.W. at the time, and very cold; but through the exertions of some of the hardy sons of Rockport, the Capt. and crew were saved. Had it been night, every soul on board must inevitably have perished. The Schr.* Daniel Webster, *from the state of Maine, laden with lumber, ran on the Londoner, a sunken ledge lying S.E. from Thatcher's Island last May, where two of her crew were washed overboard and lost; the vessel, after beating over the ledge, was run a shore on the main land near Eastern Point where two more perished, leaving but one out of five. As it was daytime when those vessels were lost, it is quite evident, that had there been buoys on the ledges, nothing of the kind would have happened. I do really hope Sir, that a bill will pass during the present session making an appropriation for placing buoys near those dangerous ledges named in our petition for that purpose. Respectfully, John Davis, LH Keeper.*

On May 26, 1849, John Davis wrote to Secretary of the Treasury William M. Meredith:

> *Sir, I have been keeper of the light on this island nearly eight years; during that time, I have strictly attended to business and eschewed politic altogether. There is now a petition in circulation in Rockport addressed to your honor, for my removal. I beg leave to state to your honor, that I have spent some money and a vast deal of labor on this island, for which I have not thus far received but small remuneration. I beg leave also to state, that I have done the state some service in my time, having served one term in our gallant*

navy. Sir, if you will have the goodness to defer my removal till the first of October next, I shall consider it a very great kindness as I shall then cheerfully resign. I wish your honor health, peace and competence, and am your most obedient servant.

Captain John Davis finally vacated the keeper position on August 18, 1849. Obviously, his request to be removed on October 1 was not granted. His eight years there were controversial, as he tried to do his best to operate a new light station that had been poorly planned, but he still had time to marry his second wife, Margaret, in 1844 at the age of sixty. His title of "Captain" may be a result of his service in the navy. Captain Davis died three years later, in July 1852.

EBENEZER POOL JR., 1807–1899

Pool served as keeper on Straitsmouth from May 3, 1852, until July 30, 1860, a total of eight years, at which time he was dismissed. He was born in Gloucester on January 2, 1807. His parents were Ebenezer Pool and Sally Howe Pool. They had ten children: Ebenezer Pool Jr., born in 1807; James Pool, 1810; Sarah A. Pool, 1812; Lyman Pool, 1814; Albert A. Pool, 1817; Francis A. Pool, 1819; Joshua Pool, 1821; George W. Pool, 1825; Eliza Pool, 1827; and Cyrus Pool, 1830.

Ebenezer Pool Jr. was listed in the 1840 census as being a mariner and a fisherman, as was his father. On December 24, 1834, he married Louisa Richardson of Gloucester. On September 15, 1835, they had a daughter named Elvira. It was also noted that on September 28, 1846, their son, Addison Everett Pool, died at three years, ten months old of infection of the bowel. By the 1850 census, Ebenezer Jr. was forty years old and listed again as a fisherman, still married to Louisa, thirty-eight; their daughter, Elvira, was now fifteen.

In the state census of 1855, Ebenezer Pool Jr. was listed as a keeper at Straitsmouth Island with his wife. In the 1860 federal census, he was reported as a light keeper, still married to Louisa, age fifty. Between 1852 and 1860, he served as lighthouse keeper on Straitsmouth, earning $350 per annum. His father, Ebenezer Sr., appeared in the 1860 census at age seventy-four, listed as "gentleman" living with two of his ten children, Sarah and Cyrus, aged forty-eight and thirty, respectively.

As we followed the census from 1870 and 1880, he was still listed as married to Louisa, and his occupation was listed as house painter. By January 17, 1885, his wife, Louisa Richardson Pool, had died one month short of age seventy-six, of consumption. Less than ten months later, on December 3, 1885, Ebenezer Jr., now seventy-five, married Louisa Colby Smith Parsons, sixty, in Rockport—his second marriage and her third.

In 1899, he was living at 18 King Street at the corner of Forest Street in Rockport. This was the location of the original ancestral family home going back four generations to the second settler in Sandy Bay, John Pool (1670–1727). John Pool built the first frame house here in 1702.

Unfortunately, we have little information of Ebenezer's life and service on Straitsmouth Light because the station logbooks of this time at the National Archives were lost to fire in the 1920s. We do know that he was the new keeper assigned one year after the building of the new lighthouse in 1851, which was established three hundred yards closer to the point on the eastern end of the island. He was also there to witness the installation of a new sixth-order Fresnel lens in the lantern room in 1857, the first Fresnel lens to be used on the island.

On March 21, 1899, Ebenezer Pool Jr. died at age ninety of bronchitis. Although he lived long and had had two marriages, we found no listings of any other children but Elvira and his son, Addison.

NEHEMIAH KNOWLTON JR., 1805–1879

Nehemiah Knowlton Jr. (1805–1879) was the third consecutive Nehemiah in six generations of American Knowltons (dating back to John Knowlton, who arrived in the American colonies as an infant in 1641). The Knowltons lived in Ipswich, Massachusetts, until Nehemiah Jr.'s father, Nehemiah Knowlton (1775–1847), married Patience Parsons (1761–1846) in Gloucester on July 26, 1797.

Nehemiah Knowlton Jr., a "shoreman" by trade, was prominent in local civil and political life and was a representative to the General Court in 1831. He is buried at Union Cemetery. His gravestone reads, "B 1/26/1806–D 12/26/1879."

Nehemiah Sr.'s wife, Patience, bore five sons when she was between the age of thirty-six and forty-three: Walter Knowlton (1798–1881), a farmer, died of heart disease at age eighty-three; Charles Knowlton (1800–1850), a yeoman, died at age fifty of cancer; Timothy Knowlton (1802–1826) died on March 1, 1826, age twenty-four; Harvey Knowlton (1803–1888) died at eighty-four of cancer; and Nehemiah Knowlton Jr., the youngest of the five children, served as Straitsmouth light keeper for fourteen years from 1866 to 1879.

Nehemiah Knowlton Jr. was twenty-three when he married eighteen-year-old Laurana Giles Tarr. She died less than two years later, on June 7, 1830, two days after the birth of their son, a third Nehemiah Knowlton. The baby died three days after his mother, on June 10, 1830, of scarlet fever. Laurana Knowlton and her baby are buried together at the Old First Parish Burying Ground in Rockport. Nehemiah Knowlton Jr.'s stone is on one side. (His second wife may have been buried elsewhere. No record has been found.) Timothy Knowlton, Nehemiah's brother, who died in 1826, is on the other side.

Six years later, on December 1, 1836, Nehemiah remarried in Portland, Maine, to Harriet Calef. Nehemiah was thirty-one and Harriet twenty-three. They settled in Sandy Bay Parish, where Nehemiah was listed by a number of occupations in official documents through the years: stonecutter in 1850, farmer in 1855, overseer of Rockport Almshouse in 1860, landlord in 1865 and light keeper in 1870.

Nehemiah and Harriet had four children: John Caleb Knowlton (1839–1907), Harriet L. Knowlton (1842–1851), Jane E. Knowlton (1850–before 1855) and Harriet "Hattie" L. Knowlton (1851–1937). Harriet married the man who would succeed her father as light keeper on Straitsmouth.

Nehemiah Knowlton had a varied life. He placed an ad in a Boston newspaper on April 17, 1823, that sparked the granite business on Cape Ann. Having cut five hundred tons of cellar and foundation stone along the shore behind the chapel at Pigeon Cove, he offered it for sale. The ad got the attention of "Major" Bates, a quarryman from Quincy, Massachusetts, home of many granite quarries. Bates set up operations in Rockport and partnered with William Torrey, who had twenty men and vessels. They branched out from Quincy to Folly Cove, having acquired the contract to supply stone for Fort Warren in Boston Harbor. Torrey established "Torrey Pit," adjacent to the Rockport Granite Company Bridge. By 1840, virtually all the granite used at government installations in Boston, Charlestown and Portsmouth navy yards was coming from there. So, the Rockport granite industry was kicked off by Nehemiah Knowlton Jr.'s first sale of those five hundred tons of Rockport granite.

Sandy Bay purchased its first fire equipment in 1829 and established an engine house in 1830 in Dock Square to house the hand pump (tub) fire engine. A company to take charge of the engine, named "Independence," was appointed on February 25, 1831, and Nehemiah Knowlton Jr. was named assistant foreman. Knowlton was also one of five negotiators assigned to a bipartisan committee in 1837 to negotiate the separation of Rockport (Sandy Bay Parish) from Gloucester, which was finally achieved with Rockport's incorporation in 1840.

By 1850, Nehemiah and Harriet Calef had three children and were about to have a fourth. Nehemiah was a stonecutter, and the family took in two young male boarders, who were quarry workers, most likely for extra money. By 1855, two of their four children had died, leaving only sixteen-year-old John and five-year-old Hattie. Nehemiah, forty-nine, and his son, John C. Knowlton, were farmers. Listed at the same address were eleven paupers (one was also labeled an "idiot"). In 1860, Nehemiah, fifty-four, and his wife, Harriet, forty-seven, lived with daughter Hattie, ten. They were overseers of the Rockport Almshouse, whose residents included seven paupers, two "idiots" and four deemed insane. John Caleb Knowlton, twenty-one, a stonecutter, was no longer in the household at this time. He was soon to join the Union army, enlisting in Company I, Massachusetts Eleventh Infantry Regiment, on July 10, 1861, and mustering out on September 6, 1862.

Nehemiah Knowlton supervised the planting of an elm tree in Dock Square in May 1859, and it stood there for many years and grew to an immense size.

In 1865, Nehemiah Knowlton, fifty-nine, and, Harriet, fifty-two, were landlords to four men and a woman of various trades. Hattie, fifteen, was a student. John Caleb Knowlton had married Margaret McInnis and started his own family in a separate household.

The following year, on December 5, 1866, Nehemiah Knowlton was appointed Straitsmouth light keeper. The 1870 federal census found him there, age sixty, accompanied by Harriet and twenty-year-old Hattie. Nehemiah was the oldest serving keeper on Straitsmouth, extending his term to fourteen years at age seventy-four. Francis (Frank) Dennis was to succeed Nehemiah as Straitsmouth keeper in 1879. (He was almost never referred to as Francis—even his marriage documents referred to him as "Frank H.")

On February 20, 1873, twenty-two-year-old Hattie Knowlton married Frank H. Dennis (1842–1925) in Rockport's Universalist Church. Nehemiah had been the Straitsmouth keeper for six years before his daughter's marriage, and he would be keeper for another six years after the event. During those years, Hattie and Frank lived in Chelsea, Massachusetts. In Gloucester, Dennis had been a mariner and a sailmaker. On his first son's birth registration, he was identified as a "Baggage Master." The Eastern Railroad Company first came to Gloucester in 1847, and then the rail was extended to Rockport in 1861. Dennis could have worked on those trains. Also, Gloucester was a center for steamship service to Maine, Boston and New York during this period. He could have worked on one of these vessels or on the docks loading luggage. It's a good guess that he worked on a steamship, having been involved in many marine businesses, listed as mariner, sailmaker and lighthouse keeper. After that, he was identified as a frame maker. This could have meant he was building fish frames called "fish flakes," used for drying fish. The docks in Gloucester had many fish flake farms to dry fish for the fish processing plants located there. Frank Dennis enlisted in New Bedford as ordinary seaman in the U.S. Navy on October 11, 1861, age nineteen, with blue eyes and light hair, at five-foot-four. He served during Civil War and was mustered out on November 20, 1864.

Nehemiah Knowlton Jr. died of heart disease on December 26, 1879, just one month short of his seventy-fourth birthday. (The death record lists his occupation as "light keeper" but does not say if he died on Straitsmouth Island or on the Rockport mainland.) Nehemiah's term of service ended on October 2, 1879 (almost three months before his death), the same day that Francis Dennis's term on Straitsmouth began. I assume that Nehemiah Knowlton's health declined in a way that allowed him to transfer responsibility for Straitsmouth Island to his son-in-law, and then lighthouse authorities went along with that choice.

The Knowlton family continued in the tradition of the sea. Joseph Lane Knowlton (1829–1900) was listed as a ship's master in 1869 aboard the Rockport Granite Company sixty-three-foot stone sloop *Ida May* and again in 1880, captaining the seventy-two-foot *New Era* sloop for the company.

THOMAS WILLARD NEWCOMB, 1859–1913

Thomas Willard Newcomb, who was named after his grandfather Thomas Newcomb (1799–1855), was born in 1859 into at least seven generations of a Cape Cod family, at least three of those generations having lived and died in Wellfleet. The census forms listed Newcomb after Newcomb households, many of them headed by mariners, master mariners and sea captains. Thomas Willard Newcomb's parents were Franklin Newcomb (1826–1862) and Mehitabel (Hattie) Collins (1828–1911). Hattie was Franklin's second wife. The first died at the age of twenty-six of consumption, leaving Franklin with two children: Angerett E. (Angie), age three, and seven-month-old Henry. In addition to raising two stepchildren, Hattie had three of her own by Franklin Newcomb: Stephen Warren Newcomb, Thomas Willard Newcomb and Sarah F. Newcomb. Sarah, the baby, died at four months old of bronchitis.

Franklin and Hattie's fourth child, Thomas Willard Newcomb, married Lucy Higgins Arnaud (1859–1936) in Wellfleet, Massachusetts, on October 19, 1893. He was thirty-four and she was thirty-three; it was a first marriage for both, and they were both from Wellfleet. She was a domestic, and he was a light keeper on Straitsmouth Island.

Thomas also served as second assistant keeper at Race Point at the tip of Cape Cod in Provincetown in 1892 and part of 1893 before being transferred to Straitsmouth. He was earning $450 per year; upon his transfer to Straitsmouth, he began at a salary of $500, which had risen to $552 by his death in 1913.

Thomas W. Newcomb had already been keeping on Straitsmouth for five and a half months before he married Lucy Arnaud that October. Their son, Henry, was born on December 1, 1894.

Hattie Newcomb was on Straitsmouth with her son Thomas, her daughter-in-law, Lucy, and her grandson, Henry, at least by 1900, staying until her death in January 1911 (suddenly, probably of heart disease). Thomas Willard Newcomb died on Straitsmouth Island at 10:00 p.m. on November 12, 1913. The doctor had been with him for four hours and judged his death to be cerebral hemorrhage, contributed to by previous hemorrhages.

Henry Warren Newcomb was sixteen when his grandmother died and nineteen when his father died, both on Straitsmouth Island. He had grown up on the island, and his father's twenty-year term of service encompassed the span of his marriage through the birth and childhood of his son. Henry is listed in the lighthouse service payroll records as keeper in 1913. He may have taken over temporarily for a year after his father had died on the island. At nineteen, he was old enough and more than likely knew the job. The 1880 federal census listed Henry and his brothers Stephen and Thomas as sailors all.

What does a boy who grows up on an island become? In 1915, Henry was living in Lynn and working as an insurance adjuster. In 1920, Henry, twenty-five and single, lived with his fifty-nine-year-old widowed mother, Lucy, in Saugus, working as an adjuster of claims for the railroad. In 1930, thirty-five-year-old Henry W. Newcomb, still single, and sixty-nine-year-old Lucy lived in New Bedford, where Henry was now a claims adjuster for an insurance company. Lucy Arnaud Newcomb died in 1936.

UP IN SMOKE

Straitsmouth Island keeper Thomas W. Newcomb's 1903 letter to lighthouse inspector Captain C.W. Bartlett started formally: "Dear Sir: The old house was totally destroyed by fire this P.M. We saved only a small part of the furniture and two cases of oil and the library." Then came the details

> *I built a fire in the kitchen stove this A.M. thinking to take some of my chickens in there to keep them warm but as there was a back draught and the stove smoked bad, I gave up the plan and mixed some paint to paint my fuel house floor and left the fire burning in the stove thinking it would burn out in a little while and started to paint the fuel house floor, in about half to three quarters of an hour Mrs. Newcomb discovered the house on fire. We did all we could to save it, but it was beyond our help.*

Newcomb added that Rockport firefighters came to their aid, but not before the house had been reduced to brick walls. Newcomb closed with the driest of understatements: "I expect to see you here very soon."

Captain Bartlett's report to the Light-House Board a few days later provided some good news. While he labeled the mishap "carelessness" on the part of the Straitsmouth keeper, he identified the building laid to ruin on June 12 as "the dwelling formerly used by the keeper of that station, situated not far from the present dwelling." Keeper Newcomb had burned down an outbuilding used for work and storage. No mention was made of the chickens.

The news story in the *Gloucester Daily Times* June 12, 1903 edition stated, "Fire at Rockport, Storehouse on Straitsmouth Island Destroyed This Afternoon—A telephone message to the Times this afternoon states that the stone building occupied as a storehouse on Straitsmouth island by the lighthouse department was on fire and with its contents would be a total loss. The building has stone ends, but the roof and sides are of wood, and in the strong wind were soon consumed."

PLAY BALL!

The islands and the mainland might have been simpatico, but the U.S. Navy knew how to go to one when the other one said no. In the early 1900s, when Rockport selectmen denied visiting naval crews permission to play baseball on Sundays, Admiral Robley Evans had a baseball diamond built on Thacher Island, which, as federal property, was unaffected by the local Blue Laws. Each ship in the North Atlantic Fleet fielded baseball teams, as well as rowing, football and swimming. In 1906, the final games of baseball championship were played between the nines of the battleships USS *Iowa* and the USS *Kentucky* on the island. The Iowa team became the 1907 fleet champs.

The Thacher ballfield was in addition to the one requested by Fleet Commander John E. Pillsbury on Straitsmouth. In July 1906, a letter from the Light-House Board "authorizes the keeper of the Straitsmouth, Mass., Light-Station to permit the use of the grounds for ball playing by the North Atlantic Fleet on the conditions mentioned and that the ground be left in good condition and that the light is not to be interfered with."

The same Light-House Board had "no objections to certain members of the keeper's family at the Straitsmouth Light-Station selling to the personnel of the North Atlantic Fleet only and on the ball ground during games only, soft drinks, tobacco, cigars, and the like." The entrepreneurial keeper was Thomas W. Newcomb, who three years earlier had burned down his barn after lighting a fire to keep his chickens warm. Their son, Henry, would have been twelve years old. What a thrill for him to be among the sailors, looking at the giant battleships anchored near the Straitsmouth shore, selling soft drinks and watching baseball with them on the island.

The Straitsmouth ballfield must have been popular with locals as well as sailors. It was the scene of a Labor Day rivalry between the International Union of Steam Engineers and the Sons of Veterans, and in September 1915, it was the site of the final game of Rockport's Sandy Bay Club. After the Giants beat the Orioles, players and their rooters settled down to a hearty clambake.

The Lone Mariner

The *Gloucester Daily Times* of June 12, 1903, reported the end of an ocean voyage by the lone mariner Elsenbraun, who landed at Rockport's lifesaving station:

> *Ludwig Elsenbraun of Boston, who possessed an ambition to gain a reputation as a lone voyager, and who set sail from Boston in a 17-foot dory for a trip across the Atlantic, is now at the Rockport lifesaving station at Straitsmouth Cove and his frail craft is riding safely at anchor offshore. Elsenbraun's adventure came to an end this morning, when seen by light keeper Newcomb of Straitsmouth lighthouse, who was coming ashore with his son. The dory voyager suddenly loomed up, coming in out of the dense fog, and asked if there was a good place to land. Mister Newcomb gave the desired information and soon Mister Bearse of the Rockport lifesaving station was on hand to help the man. He needed assistance and Captain Bearse quickly took the sailor to the station where he was cared for. Elsenbraun was suffering from exposure and after receiving some warm food and drink he quickly went to sleep. The man will remain with Captain Bearse for a day or two when all ill effects from the mental and physical strain as the result of the experience will probably be overcome. Captain Bearse showed Elsenbraun every kindness, and it is unnecessary to state that the man was deeply thankful.*

Thomas J. Creed, circa 1860–1942

Thomas J. Creed's birth falls within a six-year range between 1857 and 1863. I'm going to split the difference and say his birthdate was about 1860. Thomas J. Creed was born to James and Mary Creed (his father may have been born in Newfoundland, according to 1920 census). No birth record was found, but censuses of pre-1880 Prince Edward Island listed several Thomas Creeds (none the right age) born to Catholics of Scottish descent. Self-reported information on later censuses indicated that he immigrated to the United States in 1873, according to the 1920 census, or 1880, according to the 1930 census, and was naturalized in 1895. (The span of time between his immigration and naturalization dates could mean several things, the most logical of which is that he didn't take any steps to be naturalized until his wife, who immigrated in 1892, did.)

The earliest record that seems to be credibly our Thomas Creed comes from *Index of Surnames from the Ships and Seafarers of Atlantic Canada* (Maritime History Archive, Memorial University of Newfoundland, St. John's, Newfoundland, Canada). It lists twenty-five-year-old second mate Thomas Creed (born in 1857, Prince Edward Island) aboard the bark *Avonport*, which sailed from Liverpool, England, on February 4, 1882; made a stop in New York City, where Creed joined the crew on October 23, 1882; and ended its voyage in Rotterdam on December 7, 1882, after Creed left the vessel on December 14. He signed his papers with an "X," an indication that he could not then read or write. (The first available U.S. census in which he appears claims that he could read and write.)

A marriage record in Boston on September 20, 1889, lists Thomas Creed, thirty-three, a teamster born in Prince Edward Island to James and Mary Creed, marrying Mary McIntyre (identified on her son's death certificate as "Mary Hennessey"), thirty-one, a domestic born in St. John's Newfoundland to Thomas McIntyre and Catharine Hennessey. It was Mary's first marriage but Thomas's second. (I found no record of a first marriage in either Canada or the United States.)

Thomas J. Creed and Mary McIntyre had three children, two of whom lived into adulthood, and they adopted one child who was born in Canada: James Joseph Creed (1895–1897), Mary Ellen Creed (1897–1930), Alice Mario Creed (1901–1950) and James Edward Creed, adopted (1902–1982).

In 1905, Thomas J. Creed was working as a carpenter at Fort Strong (a military installation on the northern end of Long Island in Boston Harbor). A later census would identify him as a veteran, so he was likely a navy recruit rather than a civilian contractor.

The 1890 census is missing, and the Thomas Creed family does not appear in the 1900 or 1910 federal censuses. Despite being on Thacher Island in 1907 and 1909 (according to the list of keepers), Thomas did not appear with other keepers on Thacher Island in the federal census of 1910. Splicing together information from the keepers list, federal censuses, the Rockport/Gloucester City Directory and the birth and death records of Thomas and Mary's children, we have developed a timetable for the family.

Thomas Creed was not young when he first reported for duty on Thacher Island (May 1907 or earlier, in 1906). He was forty-four, give or take, had been married for seventeen years and had three children. He ascended the rank of assistants rapidly, moving from fourth assistant to first assistant between May 1907 and June 1909, at which time the record lists him as being "promoted." Creed was transferred to Graves Light in Boston Harbor in 1909 as a second assistant. In 1910, he became keeper at Ipswich Rear Range Light until 1912, after which he rotated back to Thacher Island as head keeper that same year.

Thomas J. Creed served as head keeper on Thacher Island for a little more than a year and a half—from April 1912 to December 12, 1913.

Something happened to create bad blood between Thomas J. Creed and his first assistant keeper, John E.H. Cook. They had previously served together on Thacher Island. In September 1906, Cook had been third assistant keeper when Thomas Creed, newly appointed to the USLHS, was fourth. Cook resigned from the light service in January 1907, allowing Creed to move up the ranks of Thacher assistant keepers. When Cook returned to the light service in September 1911, he was reassigned to the Cape Ann Light station at Thacher Island as third assistant keeper under his old boss Addison Tarr, who had been head keeper for twenty-eight years. When Tarr retired in April 1912, Thomas J. Creed returned to Thacher Island and took his place as head keeper. Maybe that elevation of someone he knew as a fourth assistant to head keeper created resentment in Cook.

Meanwhile, there was another drama playing out on Straitsmouth Island. Thomas Newcomb, the longest-serving Straitsmouth keeper in its history (more than twenty years), had had a series of cerebral vascular accidents, the last of which would kill him on November 12, 1913. It is unclear who was managing that light station in the fall of 1913. Henry W. Newcomb, his son of nineteen, may have temporarily filled in. On many light stations, family members often filled in if the keeper were ill, incapacitated or died. It's possible that Thacher's head keeper, Thomas Creed, felt the need to monitor and/or assist the Newcombs, which means he was frequently away from Thacher Island.

That, more than jealousy, resentment or natural antagonism between the two men, might explain the extraordinary demand by the then first assistant made on the head keeper. On October 23, 1913, Creed wrote in the keeper's log, "Mr. Cook, 1st Asst. wanted journals. I refused." A later entry noted, "1st Asst tantalizing me in fog sig, 50 minutes." That month, John Cook left the station one day and didn't tell Creed where he was going (perhaps to Boston to file a complaint). The second assistant, Howard Carter, did the same thing on two occasions. Twenty days after Cook's absence, Lighthouse Inspector R.H. Goddard came to the station and found it in fair condition but told keeper Creed to get to work scaling and painting the towers.

Inspector Goddard returned on December 3, 1913, apparently to tell them how the tension on the island could be relieved (Newcomb's death having left an opening on Straitsmouth). In a December 4, 1913 journal entry, Keeper Creed wrote, "1st Asst Cook attempt assault with danger weapon, 2nd asst Carter with oar." On December 6, the third assistant, Cobb, left the station and did not report his return. On the ninth, Keeper Creed and his family packed up and on December 12, 1913, moved to Straitsmouth Island. Cook took charge of the Cape Ann Station as acting head keeper, although he was not officially appointed to the position until mid-March 1914.

Transfer from Thacher to Straitsmouth came with a substantial pay cut from $780 per month for the head keeper position on Thacher to $500 per month on Straitsmouth, but it must have suited the Creed family well enough. They settled into the Straitsmouth station and stayed there for the next four years. John E.H. Cook may have felt momentarily relieved and perhaps even triumphant at the removal of Thomas Creed, but he would have his own problems with insubordinate assistants and would eventually choose to take a pay cut to transfer to Straitsmouth himself.

When the Creeds left Straitsmouth Island, in January 1918, they returned to Boston, where Thomas J. Creed, now in his mid- to late fifties, found work in a variety of positions from mate and boatswain to ship's carpenter aboard schooners and steamships that made trips to, among other places, Suriname, Cuba, Honduras and Colombia. Existing manifests span the years between 1918 and 1931.

Many of the vessels he crewed on were part of United Fruit Company's fleet of banana boats traveling to its main port in Tela, Honduras. Two of the United Fruit ships he was on as carpenter included the SS *Maravi* and SS *San Blas*. His son, James, had enlisted in the U.S. Navy, probably in early 1920, served seven years and became, again, a merchant seaman like his father, serving on at least one voyage with his father in February 1930, sailing on the SS *San Blas* from Boston to Tela, Honduras, and back. Thomas J. Creed, fifty-six, was a carpenter, and James E. Creed, twenty-eight, was a quartermaster.

The 1920 census found the Creed family at 101 Old Harbor Street in Boston. Thomas J. Creed, fifty-six, was a sailor for a steamship line. He was on the manifest of the SS *Esparta*, sailing from Limon, Costa Rica, to New Orleans as a boatswain. Mary J. Creed, his wife, was also fifty-six; daughter Mary E. Creed, twenty-one, was a stenographer for a fire insurance company; Alice M. Creed, nineteen, was a stenographer for a life insurance company; and James E. Creed, like his father, was a sailor for a steamship company.

In the 1930 census, Thomas was a carpenter employed in "shipbuilding." The last reported manifest in 1931 indicates that he was on the SS *San Blas* from Tela, Honduras, that arrived on January 25, 1931. Thomas was later reported on the SS *San Blas* from Puerto Castilla, Honduras, to Boston, arriving on November 9, 1931. He would have been seventy years old at this time.

Thomas J. Creed died in Arlington, Massachusetts, in 1942, age eighty-five, give or take.

JOHN (JACK) E.H. COOK, 1879–1940

John W. Scott Cook (John E.H. Cook's father) was born on October 14, 1855, in Dover, New Hampshire, and died on November 8, 1915, on Thacher Island. The housepainter, who lived in Haverhill, Massachusetts, married Mary Ann Mahon on July 17, 1876, in Haverhill. They had two children: Josephine Mary Cook, born on December 23, 1877, and John Edwin Herbert Cook, born on February 1, 1879. According to family lore, Josephine Cook died giving birth to her son. In 1880, J.W.S. Cook and his two children, ages three and one, were living in Atkinson, New Hampshire. John W.S. Cook was a painter and a paper hanger. His son, John E.H. Cook probably worked with him at some point.

In 1896, at the age of seventeen, John E.H. Cook moved to Newburyport, where he stayed in Mary J. Dugan's boardinghouse. He worked for Perkins Lumber Company for eight years and joined his boss Captain A.G. Perkins's regiment (Company A, Eighth Regiment, Massachusetts Volunteer Militia), bound for the Spanish-American War. He was stationed in Chickamauga, Georgia, then at Camp Hamilton, Lexington, Kentucky, before leaving on the transport *Michigan* for Matanzas, Cuba. He arrived in Cuba on January 13, 1899, after the war had ended, but he served as part of the Army of the Occupation until April 4, 1899, when he left on the transport *Meade* for Boston and was mustered out on April 28, 1899.

During that time, there was little food and much sickness among the troops. John E.H. Cook was in a sick ward for more than thirty days in Lexington, from August to November 1898, with typhoid fever. On February 4, 1899 (while in Cuba), he sought medical care for acute diarrhea. He would later receive a government pension for a "left varicocele" (an enlargement of a vein in the scrotum).

John E.H. Cook mustered out with $86.18 in pay but remained in Company A, Eighth Regiment, Second Brigade, headquartered in Salem, Massachusetts, until he completed his two-year term on April 28, 1900.

He went back to work for Perkins Lumber Company in Newburyport. On September 30, 1903, when he was twenty-four, he married Emma Marie Ducharme (1883–1953), age twenty. She was originally from Warwick, Quebec, but had moved to Amesbury with her family in 1887 and then to Newburyport. She was a seamstress and, at the time of the wedding, a shoe stitcher for E.P. Dodge Manufacturing of Newburyport. A difficult pregnancy produced twin boys on November 13, 1904: John Edwin Herbert Cook Jr. and Daniel Henry Scott Cook.

In 1905, they owned a houseboat that John had built himself, and they kept it moored in an inlet at Plum Island. Everyone was happy and healthy until August 1905, when the family's lives, and fortunes seemed to suddenly shift. John left his job with Perkins Lumber and sold the houseboat, and they moved in with Emma's family. His son John Jr. died on August 22, 1905, at the age of nine months, of amebic enterocolitis. Cook bought a plot at Elmwood Cemetery in Bradford, Massachusetts, where the entire family (except a later son, Donald) would eventually be buried.

John E.H. Cook on Graves and Thacher

Three days after his son's death, Cook's new job went into effect. He was appointed first assistant on the newly built Graves Light Station in the outermost part of Boston Harbor. He had been offered the job by a man he had befriended in Newburyport, Elliott C. Hadley, who was signed on as head keeper of Graves. There were two other assistants. The family moved to Winthrop, from which Graves Light was but a six-mile boat ride.

On March 6, 1906, fourteen-month-old Daniel died of "laboring pneumonia." John Cook took leave to be with his wife and then returned to Graves Light ten days later on March 16, 1906. He soon received a new assignment at Cape Ann Light Station, Thacher Island, effective September 15, 1906. He was third assistant of five keepers on the island: head keeper Addison Franklin Tarr; James T. Allison, first assistant; Francis J. Cook (no relation), second; John E.H. Cook, third; and Thomas J. Creed, fourth. Creed would later be named head keeper.

John and Emma lived in the house at the North Light, along with Creed, who had three children (Mary Ellen, nine; Alice, five; and James, four). According to the Cook family biography, Addison Franklin Tarr and his son, Frank Tarr, lived at the South Light, along with first assistant Allison and his wife, who had three children (James, fifteen; Frank, thirteen; and Ester, eight).

John E.H. Cook resigned from the light service in January 1907, and he and Emma moved back to Newburyport, where he resumed his job as a foreman at Perkins Lumber Company. By July 1907, Emma was again pregnant, another difficult one, with much time spent in bed. Emma gave birth to her third son, Donald Theodore Cook, on March 24, 1908, in Newburyport but didn't name him and reportedly had a hard time loving him. Relatives finally stepped in and named him Donald.

In July 1910, they moved to Lynn to be near Emma's mother and three of her sisters, probably because she was again pregnant. She delivered a stillborn girl on May 17, 1911, in Lynn. Emma liked being around family, but John liked being around the sea, so he reapplied for a light keeping position, one of which opened on September 22, 1911, when Wilford G. Burt was transferred from the Cape Ann Light Station. Eugene N. Larsen had been assigned to the island on September 1, 1910, along with Charles B. Hill on September 6—all were early members of a service that was transitioning to a professional organization. They were a new breed of "career men."

Emma came to Thacher with a piano, which was taken to the island on a lighthouse tender ship and transferred to a smaller boat and then to a flatcar between rocks at the water's edge; it was then hauled up by a winch line. They again lived in the North House (which would burn to the ground in 1935). John was thirty-two, Emma twenty-eight and Donald three and a half. They would remain on Thacher for six and a half years.

John E.H. Cook was promoted throughout those years from third assistant in 1911 to second and first by 1912, acting keeper in 1913 and finally head keeper on March 15, 1914. Tensions were evident between Cook and Thomas Creed, as related earlier in the section on Creed. On December 9, 1913, Keeper Creed and his family packed up, later moving to Straitsmouth. Cook took charge of the Cape Ann Station on December12, 1913, and was officially appointed head keeper in mid-March 1914.

For Emma, life on Thacher and away from her family was lonely at first, but her family visited often. She loved to cook and sing and took to rowing, standing up, to the mainland. According to Emma's youngest sister Louise, John was a "kidder" who would rock the boat to scare them. He smoked

The Cook family—John, Emma and son Donald—in 1911; he was third assistant in this photo and became principal keeper in 1914. *David Cook.*

constantly, cigar or pipe, and was a "wonderful person," as was Emma, who was very sociable. Sister Flora visited most often. They sang and got others to sing with them.

Donald started school in September 1914, boarding on the mainland during the school week. Other children on the island at that time included Howard and Alice Carter's daughters, Nellie (born on May 11, 1903) and Mildred (March 25, 1905); they were five and three years older than Donald, who was born in 1908. The Carters came to Thacher Island in June 1913 and spent four years on the island. The children boarded at Mrs. Ben Dobson's house at 17 South Street (now no. 19). The government allowed one dollar per day per child. Sometimes they were ferried to the island by Emerson Haskell, who operated an outdoor shore dinner restaurant in Loblolly Cove as well as a boat rental business. In bad weather, the children sometimes didn't get back to the island for "weeks and months"; weather also stranded them on the island so they couldn't get back to school.

John Cook's father (in Bradford, Massachusetts) visited, usually alone. On Sunday, November 7, 1915, the sixty-one-year-old became ill and died at 7:30 a.m. The Straitsmouth Coast Guard was alerted by a blast of the foghorn between 3:00 p.m. and 5:00 p.m. Captain Aubin and his crew responded in rough seas in an unpowered lifeboat. They couldn't land on Thacher until Monday, and when they were leaving the island at 9:00 a.m., they called Captain King of the Dolliver's Neck Station, who towed the Straitsmouth lifeboat ashore, along with Keeper Cook and the body of his father. According to Donald Cook, his father was upset that John W.S. Cook had visited when he knew his health was so bad, but perhaps that was the reason he came. The official cause of death was chronic endocarditis.

Keepers got thirty days leave of absence per year provided that, if necessary, they procured substitutes at their own expense. In June 1917, John's stepbrother, Scott L. Cook, was a substitute for assistant keeper Davis. On July 22, 1917, John E.H. Cook was commended for assistance rendered to two fishermen from the schooner *Commonwealth* who had been lost in a fog.

In April 1917, during World War I, keepers were given the additional assignment of submarine lookout, but on October 13, 1917, five men from the Naval Reserves were assigned to that duty on the island. They lived in "the spare house," which was converted to a small barracks. Now John E.H. Cook had the challenge of five extra men working in the same space as the light keepers. Seaman Jeffrey helped a keeper clean the stone deck in the South Tower, which led Cook to order all seamen to do their watches from the parapets in decent weather (log entry, October 26, 1917) to avoid further mixing of duties.

Tensions flared up from time to time, notably with assistant keepers Huse and second assistant Boothby. In 1917, Boothby was insubordinate and left the island to go to Boston to complain. He was ordered to return to Thacher Island.

On July 20, 1917, Howard Carter transferred to Graves Light Station. Emma Cook and Alice Carter had been good friends and even took a trip to New York City together in 1914. This also meant their children, Donald's companions, left the island.

THE COOKS ON STRAITSMOUTH ISLAND

In December 1917, Thomas J. Creed resigned as head keeper of Straitsmouth, and John accepted the position on January 10, 1918, despite a pay cut from $904 to $552 per year. He served there until at least November 1923, maybe as late as 1925. The reasons for requesting/accepting the transfer may have been twofold.

First, the job of head keeper on Thacher Island had become too much for John Cook. In 1911 (when he was a third assistant), the number of keepers had been reduced from five to four. A few months after the Cooks left Thacher, the Department of Commerce and Labor returned the number of keepers to five, but during Cook's time as head keeper the increased workload was done by fewer men, which meant more difficulty getting time on the mainland. He also had to keep an eye on five naval reservists over whom there may have been ambiguous supervisory control.

Second, nine-and-a-half-year-old Donald was now the only child on the island. He made the long walk alone from the drop point at Loblolly Cove to his boardinghouse. Straitsmouth Island, closer to town, allowed him to be taken into the harbor, and it allowed Emma more freedom to be involved with Donald's schooling and see her friends in town. (When Donald Cook was in his teens, he and his mother were in several recitals, separately and together. She sang, and he played the piano and sang.) It was also more convenient for friends to visit Emma, which they often did.

Josephine Thibeault, Emma's niece, lost her first child seven weeks after birth (September 7, 1920). Emma hosted her on the island for emotional rest and sympathy. "Aunt Emma knew how I felt and what I was going through, she has gone through it twice herself. She knew what I needed."

While the Cooks were on Straitsmouth, a movie, *Out of the Fog*, was made on the island. The plot involved a man who died in an accident; in a fit of despair, the woman who loved him threw herself off the lighthouse. A dummy was used, and Eastern Point Light was substituted for Straitsmouth Light. Emma cooked for the cast and crew and made friends with several who visited the Cooks over the years. The *Gloucester Daily Times* ran an article on May 13, 1919, about the film, "Movie Show of Great Local Interest." It reported that the movie was shot in Rockport Harbor, Old Garden Beach, Gully Point, Straitsmouth, the breakwater and Eastern Point Light.

While Emma seems to have made the best of being a keeper's wife, she moved to the mainland after three or four years on Straitsmouth (in about 1921–22) and found a lot on Norwood Avenue in Rockport. She and John took a loan from the Granite Savings Bank and built two houses on the property. (John appears to have done the work while off the island, with Donald assisting.)

Donald went to Gloucester High School on Dale Avenue through his junior year. Meanwhile, in 1925, Lizzie Belle (Isabelle, the widow of John's father) moved to Rockport with her son, Scott Longfellow Cook (the half-brother who had subbed for an assistant keeper on Thacher). Scott had been a member of the Merchant Marines (sailing to the Philippines) and had served on the second *Kearsarge* in 1916. (The battleship, launched in March 1898 and named after the first *Kearsarge*, sailed around the world with the Great White Fleet, came to Rockport several times for maneuvers, participated in World War I, was converted to a heavy-crane ship in 1920 and then was sold for scrapping on August 9, 1955.)

John retired as keeper before 1925 (probably December 1924 because George F. Woodman Jr. started his Straitsmouth keepership on January 1, 1925). John E.H. Cook worked alongside his half-brother, Scott, as a carpenter/contractor. He did much work for the Straitsmouth Inn (owned by a Mrs. Wilkerson). In about 1925–26, he was a part of a group that pooled its money to purchase a house in Ross Corner, Maine, where the group vacationed.

Emma was active in Rockport clubs and the church (she belonged to St. Joachim) and played the piano for silent movies. She made pottery and went on trips with friends. Donald went to the Salem Commercial

School and worked as a fisherman and for the Rockport Tool Company. (He met Jeannette E. Darsigny aboard his tool company boss's yacht.) He became a fireman aboard lighthouse tenders and lightships, and when the light service was absorbed by the Coast Guard, he joined the Coast Guard Service.

John E.H. Cook died on Sunday evening, October 27, 1940, at the U.S. Naval Hospital in Chelsea, Massachusetts (at the age of sixty-one, just like his father), of cerebral hemorrhage, hypertension and arterial sclerosis.

Emma, who had rheumatoid arthritis, found her cottage too difficult to keep up. She sold it in 1944, fixed up John's old workshop to live in and rented her former home. She lived with her son, Donald, on Norwood Avenue for a short time but ended her years in a convalescent home, bedridden except for brief mobility on crutches. She died on February 8, 1953 (at age sixty-nine or seventy), of a cerebral hemorrhage.

David Cook, John E.H. Cook's grandson, who provided much of this information, was sixteen years old when his grandmother Emma died in 1953. David is a Roman Catholic priest.

Hoyt P. Smith, 1900–1973

Charles Francis Smith, Francis C. Smith and Frank Smith (1873–1947) all appear to be the same man, a lifelong resident of Jonesport, Maine, and the son of Henry E. Smith (1848–1934), another lifelong resident of Jonesport, and Sarah Augusta Foss (1853–1925), a woman from Machiasport, twenty miles along the coast. Frank was one of eleven siblings, seven of whom lived into adulthood, so when the twenty-two-year-old stonemason married twenty-year-old Agnes Viola Farnsworth (1875–1946) in 1895, they lost no time producing eight children of their own.

Frank was a surf fisherman in 1900. He eventually became a carpenter in a boat shop and was listed that way in the census through 1940 when he was sixty-eight. His children all worked in the area in a clam and sardine factory, a major employer in Jonesport.

This was, to all appearances, a hardworking Yankee family centered so firmly in Jonesport that Greenwood Cemetery in that town reads like a genealogy of the Smith family. (His parents lie there, as do Frank and his wife, at least seven of his eleven siblings, six of his children and a cenotaph for the seventh, their spouses and many of their children.) Frank was a fisherman and then a boat carpenter; his children worked early, first in the clam and sardine factories and then in boatbuilding. But Frank and Agnes owned their own house, and it was commodious enough to take in their grown children and grandchildren when required.

This was a family blessed with a measure of longevity. Frank was fifty-two when he lost his seventy-one-year-old mother in March 1925 and sixty-one when he lost his eighty-five-year-old father in August 1934. That he lost his thirty-three-year-old son Charles F. Smith the following year, in November 1935, is still a relatively contained loss of one in seven children in the years before the discovery of penicillin.

He lost a second son, his youngest, in the Battle of Okinawa in 1945. Though tragic, even that was a statistically reasonable loss in a family filled with those who served in World War II, but it may have been the beginning of Frank's final slide. Frank's brother died that June; and Frank's wife, Agnes, died the following March 1946. The following year, on November 21, 1947, Frank passed away at the age of seventy-four.

Children of Frank Smith and Agnes Farnsworth include Edith (Etta), Amelia Smith (1896–1963), Oscar Alonzo Smith (1897–1992), Henry Vinton Smith (1899–1989), Hoyt Philmore Smith (1900–1973), Charles F. Smith (1902–1935), Leland J. Smith (1905–1978) and Melzer Rupert Smith (1911–1945).

Hoyt Philmore Smith (1900–1973) was keeper on Thacher from 1925 to 1927, transferred to Straitsmouth 1928 until 1933. He was the last federal light keeper on Straitsmouth. *USLHS.*

Hoyt P. Smith, the fourth of Frank and Agnes Farnsworth Smith's seven children, was born on August 6, 1900, in Jonesport, Maine, just after the enumeration of the 1900 federal census. His World War I draft registration listed him as eighteen years old, a common laborer employed by Emery Farnsworth of Jonesport, Maine. (Emery was not one of his mother's siblings but was probably a member of the extended Smith-Farnsworth family of Jonesport.)

Hoyt married Velora Jane Lamson (1903–1997) in Jonesport on November 15, 1919, when he was a nineteen-year-old laborer and she was sixteen. He was out of his parents' household by the 1920 federal census but still in Jonesport and still a laborer when his first son, Philmore Harland Smith (1920–2011), was born on May 10, 1920. Hoyt was working as a fisherman in Jonesport when his daughter, Ruth Leone Smith, was born on July 22, 1922. Third child Coleman F. Smith was born on July12, 1924.

Hoyt Smith had a wife and three children under the age of five with him when he began his job as third assistant keeper on Thacher Island on July 20, 1925. He was promoted to second assistant keeper in April 1926 and to first assistant keeper on April 8, 1927. He was transferred to Straitsmouth Island sometime after that, most likely in January 1928, to directly succeed George F. Woodman. The 1930 federal census showed the household on Straitsmouth Island to include Hoyt, twenty-nine; Velora, twenty-six; Philmore, nine; Ruth, seven; and Coleman, five. They stayed on Straitsmouth just short of six years (January 1928–October 1933) until Hoyt was transferred to Ashtabula, Ohio, on October 10, 1933, where he served as third assistant keeper of the Ashtabula Light on the shores of Lake Erie.

Lighthouse management changed radically in the 1930s. In 1932, the light was extinguished in Thacher's North Tower as a cost-cutting measure, leaving only the light in the South Tower for the keepers to maintain. In 1933, Straitsmouth's light was swapped out for an electrified incandescent light connected to an automated time switch, Hoyt Smith was transferred to the Ashtabula Light Station in Ohio as third assistant keeper and the reduced staff of keepers on Thacher was charged with making periodic visits to Straitsmouth to supervise the island and its light. Straitsmouth Island was sold to a private party in 1941 after the light station was deactivated and the crews moved to Gap Cove Life-Saving Station.

The Ashtabula Light Station would eventually meet the same fate—automation and deacquisition. The lighthouse sits at the end of a long breakwater overlooking Ashtabula Harbor, where the Ashtabula River flows into Lake Erie. The original 1836 structure had been rebuilt, and by Hoyt Smith's day, it had a fourth-order Fresnel lens. Ashtabula Light was the last manned light on Lake Erie. It was maintained by the USCG until 1973, when it was turned over to the City of Ashtabula.

The 1934 city directory for Ashtabula, Ohio, listing "Smith, Hoyt P. (Velora J), watchman, h 1653 w 6th," raises questions. There was housing at the lighthouse. Why didn't the family live there? Why is Hoyt referred to as a watchman? Was it a second job? The 1940 federal census, which found Hoyt on Boon Island, Maine, listed his previous residence (April 1, 1935) as Ashtabula, but the 1937 city directory did not list the Hoyt Smith family as residents of Ashtabula, so they most likely moved back to Maine between mid-1935 and mid-1937.

Hoyt P. Smith and Velora Jane Lamson had six children: Philmore Harland Smith (born in 1920), Ruth Leone Smith (1922), Coleman F. Smith (1924), Mary Smith (1930), Hoyt Evans Smith (1934) and Charles Smith (1937).

In the 1940 census for Boon Island, Maine, Hoyt, thirty-nine, light keeper, was for the first time designated USCG, at a salary of $1,440. His family was not with him (they had settled in York Village, Maine, although I could find none of the family in the 1940 federal census). Those with Hoyt on Boon Island included Harry McClure, forty-six; Henry S. Brown, thirty-five; and Henry's wife, Evelyn Brown, thirty-five.

It's not hard to see why the Smith family preferred to stay on the mainland. Despite its impressive height (at 133 feet, exclusive of the light, it is the tallest lighthouse in New England), Boon Island Light sits six miles off the coast of Maine on a piece of totally vegetation-free land that is, at low tide, 300 by 700 feet in area and 14 feet above sea level. During storms, the sea washes across the island.

It is unlikely that Hoyt himself lasted long on Boon Island. Except for one keeper (William W. Williams, who lasted twenty-seven years), keepers arrived and left in brisk succession. Boon Island appears to have been Hoyt Smith's last lighthouse posting. He and Velora spent the rest of their lives in York Village, Maine, where he died on March 8, 1973, at the age of seventy-two. He was buried with his parents and siblings at Greenwood Cemetery in Jonesport with a military gravestone that identified him as BMCX U.S. Coast Guard (perhaps Boatswain Mate Chief Petty Officer X?).

Velora Lamson Smith survived her husband by twenty-four years and died in York Village on March 12, 1997, at the age of ninety-three. She joined the extended Smith family at Jonesport's Greenwood Cemetery.

First Lighthouse Keepers of the Modern Era

Although Hoyt Smith was the last official light keeper on Straitsmouth employed by the U.S. Lighthouse Service, in June 2019 the first civilian lighthouse keeper was installed by the Town of Rockport's Thacher/Straitsmouth Town Committee to begin the summer schedule of light keepers for the first time in eighty-six years since Hoyt Smith left in 1933.

First civilian keepers Joe Napolitano and Peggy Flanagan, heading toward the Straitsmouth lighthouse in June 2019. *From the* Gloucester Daily Times, *Paul Bilodeau.*

Joseph Napolitano and his wife, Peggy Flanagan, were honored as the first of many volunteer keepers who would serve on Straitsmouth during the summer months from June until September. They are the first of several sets of volunteer keepers scheduled to spend a week or two over the summer welcoming visitors and work crews to the island. They will be busy clearing and managing the walking trails, allowing the public to climb the lighthouse and making ongoing repairs and improvements. Joe and Peggy moved into the newly restored seven-room keeper house in June 2019, which Joe and his team from his contracting company, NAPCO Inc., had spent four years restoring and rehabilitating. The 1878 Victorian house needed major repairs both internally and externally, including all new interior walls, new floors, complete replacement of all plumbing and new electrical system now powered by solar panels. Even a composting toilet in the new bathroom has added to the environmentally reduced carbon footprint. A propane gas refrigerator, a dryer and a special triple-filtered water system that gathers water from the roof and stores it in the two original (newly lined) three-thousand-gallon cisterns completes the setup. All gray water is processed through this unique system, providing recycled potable drinking water.

Napolitano specializes in historic preservation. He led the renovation of the keeper house on Thacher in the early 2000s and has worked on historic buildings such as the House of Seven Gables in Salem and the Sargent House in Gloucester throughout his career as a contractor. In his early days, he worked on the reconstruction of the USS *Constitution* in Boston and the *Charles W. Morgan*, the last of the great whaling ships in Mystic, Connecticut.

When asked if the house could be saved, Joe said, "Anything can be saved." Joe was also quoted as saying, "Anything can be repaired....Only life can't be." So begins a new era of lighthouse keeping on Straitsmouth into the twenty-first century.

Keepers of Straitsmouth Light Station, 1835–1933

Keeper	*Annual Salary*	*Appointed*	*Vacated*	*Reason Vacated*	*Years Served*
Benjamin Andrews	$350	9/1/1835	8/15/1840	died	5
Captain John Davis	$350	7/1/1841	8/18/1849	resigned	8
Henry F. Low	$350	8/17/1849	1850	?	1
Sylvester Pearce	$350	7/30/1850	1852	transferred	2
Ebenezer Pool Jr.	$350	5/3/1852	7/30/1860	removed	8
Sylvester Pearce	$350	7/30/1860	10/18/1861	removed	1
John S. Wheeler	$350	10/18/1861	10/8/1866	resigned	5
William Cunningham	$350	10/8/1866	12/5/1866	removed	2 mos.
Nehemiah Knowlton	$500	12/5/1866	10/2/1879	resigned	14
Frank H. Dennis	$500	11/15/1879	6/13/1883	removed	4
Walter S. Rogers	$500	6/20/1883	7/20/1892	transferred	9
Walter S. Thompson	$500	7/12/1892	4/24/1893	resigned	1
Thomas W. Newcomb	$500	5/1/1893	11/12/1913	died	20

Keeper	*Annual Salary*	*Appointed*	*Vacated*	*Reason Vacated*	*Years Served*
Henry W. Newcomb*		11/1913	12/1913	replaced father	1 mo.
Thomas Creed	$500	1/1/1914	01/31/1918	resigned	5
John E.H. Cook	$552	2/1/1918	1923–25?	resigned	7
George F. Woodman Jr.	$1,260	1/1/1925	1928	transferred	3
Hoyt P. Smith	$1,200	1/16/1928	10/10/1933	transferred	6

*Henry W. Newcomb filled in after his father Thomas's sudden death, November 12, 1913.

Source: National Archives, Waltham, Massachusetts.

Chapter 10

PRIVATE OWNERS OF STRAITSMOUTH ISLAND, 1941–1967

The process of the federal government closing the island took seven years from the first quiet rumblings of a closure to the controversy about selling the island or renting it to the final decision to sell it to a New York playwright in 1941. The island passed to seven different private owners from 1941 to 1967.

Before the first sale to Glenn Wilson of New York, the government agreed to lease the island to a man by the name of Edward Knowlton of Cambridge, Massachusetts, to occupy the "Straitsmouth Lighthouse Reservation." (Not sure if he was related to Keeper Nehemiah Knowlton). He leased the island from July 1, 1934, until October 1, 1934, for $20 per month, payable in advance. There were rumors around that he wanted to open a restaurant there or just have a summer vacation house at little expense. Either way, little ever came of it, and the government finally decided to sell it. It was put out for bid in May 1941, with an opening bid price of $3,200 by the Real Estate Section, Public Buildings Administration, Federal Works Agency, in Washington D.C. On June 7, 1941, Glenn Wilson won the bidding with a bid of $3,050 over four other bids ranging from $525 to $2,150. The local newspaper, the *Rockport Daily*, on June 29, 1941, reported, "He bought a skiff so he could provide his own ferry across the 300 feet stretch of open water between the mainland and his Robinson Crusoe abode."

GLENN WILSON, 1941–46

Glenn Wilson was a thirty-five-year-old Manhattan playwright who wrote small plays for radio broadcasts. He was a nautical type, sailing his forty-seven-foot yawl *Saga*. He discovered Straitsmouth during one of his many sails along the eastern seaboard. The *Rockport Daily* reported one month later when Wilson arrived at the island that "his only company were some 500 Belgian hares that roamed the place." Wilson frequently invited his New York friends to stay with him to see what living like a hermit was like, even though there was no water and kerosene lantern lamps were his only source of illumination. His taxes that first year were $204.

Wilson sold the island to Stanley Littlefield on February 5, 1946, apparently disappointed with living on an island with no utilities and nothing but rabbits to watch.

STANLEY LITTLEFIELD, 1946–48

Littlefield owned it until February 17, 1948, when he sold it to Edward Wendell, a real estate investor who had formed the Rockport Pier Company down on Bearskin Neck. Stanley Littlefield only owned the island for two years and never did anything with it. Wendell owned many lots on the neck, having bought out businesses there. In December 1950, he transferred ownership from himself to the Rockport Pier Company, likely for tax purposes. Wendell bought a parcel of land on Marmion Way called Stonehaven in 1947 from Arthur Park, the co-owner of Durgin-Park, the famous restaurant in Boston. This purchase included the large home that eventually became the Seacrest Manor.

EDWARD NELSON WENDELL, 1948–54

Wendell had family ties to Rockport going back to his relative Charles J. Wendell, who was the keeper on Thacher Island from 1891 to 1894. This information came from genealogical records provided by Roger Wendell, who lived here in Rockport for many years and related the information to the author in 2006.

The original Wendell family in America consisted of three brothers, Charles, George and Robert, who came from Sweden in the 1860s. Charles had a son, the future keeper Charles Julius, born in 1865. Charles Julius was married to Etta Andrews.

Roger recalled meeting Charles in 1957 at his home in Ipswich. Charles was the first cousin of George Edward Wendell (Roger's grandfather) and therefore Roger's first cousin twice removed. Roger met him when he was ninety-two, when Charles turned over to Roger's father (Edward Nelson Wendell) the original family seal, battle flag and proclamation of ennoblement from King Carl XII of Sweden, who was a cousin. The direct ancestor was King Karl VIII, the twelfth great-grandfather of Charles Julius. Charles was not an heir to the throne; however, he was a descendant.

Roger told us that after leaving the island, Charles was engaged as a general repairman, working at schools at least part of the time. Roger's father, Edward Nelson Wendell, was a prominent engineer and landowner in Rockport. Edward graduated from Gloucester High School and MIT and became the leading radio engineer and one of the leading electrical engineers in the world. He bought the Cable House on Norwood Avenue in the 1930s and converted it from an office building to a private summer residence, adding the cottage on the Atlantic Avenue side of the property for his parents. (This was the cable station office and workshop of the Commercial Cable Company, which operated the Mackay-Bennett transatlantic cable that ran from Pebble Beach in Rockport to Nova Scotia and across the Atlantic to Valentia, Ireland.) In the 1940s, he sold the Cable House.

Edward then bought a house on Marmion Way that became Seacrest Manor. About the same time, he bought Straitsmouth Island from Stanley Littlefield; the Rockport Pier Company; Hodgkin's Wharf, which he later named Tuna Wharf; and the North, South and Middle Roads of Bearskin Neck. He then gave the roads to the town and gave it the land for the launching ramp in Dock Square, as the town had no access to its own waterfront.

He then went to Japan for a year to rebuild its communication facilities after the war, while Roger's mother, Eunice, oversaw the reconstruction of Tuna Wharf. After several years in Argentina, running ITT's South American operations, he retired to Rockport at what was then 55 Marmion Way.

The Wendells established shops on Tuna Wharf which were the first on Bearskin Neck, except for Lew Whitney's Pewter Shop. This story brings us full circle as to the intriguing relationships of Thacher keepers, Rockport residents, the kings of Sweden and owners of Straitsmouth Island.

ARTHUR COLTON, 1954

The Wendells' Rockport Pier Company sold the island to Arthur Colton on October 20, 1954, and he immediately resold it to William Francis Gibbs on October 29 that year. We are not sure why this transaction took place or who Colton was.

WILLIAM FRANCIS GIBBS, 1954–64

Gibbs was a renowned naval architect who directed the mass production of cargo ships for the United States during World War II, including the famous Liberty ships, of which 2,751 were built. In partnership with his brother, Frederic Herbert Gibbs, he designed the passenger liner SS *United States* in 1952.

Gibbs was born in Philadelphia in 1886, followed his own curriculum of science and engineering at Harvard, where he studied plans for British battleships in his dorm room but left without a degree, and then attended Columbia Law School in 1911–13, receiving a Master of Arts in economics.

He and his brother started their own naval architecture firm, Gibbs Brothers, in 1922, renamed Gibbs & Cox in 1929. During the war, Gibbs & Cox created plans for thousands of American warships, including destroyers, LST landing craft, minesweepers, tankers, cruisers, liberty ships and more. Some 74 percent of all American naval vessels built during the war were of Gibbs & Cox design.

Their first major contract was to convert the former German liner *Vaterland* into the American luxury liner SS *Leviathan*. When shipbuilders Blohm + Voss asked for more than $1 million for the original plans, Gibbs decided to draw his own. Between 100 and 150 draftsmen documented the existing ship and designed its new layout. After rebuilding at Newport News, the *Leviathan* ultimately became one of the era's most successful luxury liners.

The Gibbses designed a series of trim white-hulled ocean liners for the Matson Lines service to Hawaii, starting with the SS *Malolo* in 1925 and continuing with the SS *Monterey* and SS *Mariposa* in 1931 and the SS *Lurline* in 1932. The Grace Line contracted with Gibbs & Cox for four smaller nine-thousand-ton ocean liners in 1930, receiving the *Santa Rosa*, *Santa Paula*, *Santa Lucia* and *Santa Elena* in 1932. Gibbs & Cox also designed the SS *America* for the United States Lines, which was completed

William Francis Gibbs, renowned naval architect, was the last private owner of Straitsmouth before his brother donated it to Mass Audubon in 1967. *Author's collection.*

in 1940 after war had already broken out. All nine of these ships served as troopships in World War II.

After World War II, the Gibbs brothers began the design for the one-thousand-foot ocean liner SS *United States*. On its maiden voyage in 1952, it became the fastest ship to cross the Atlantic Ocean. It was the largest liner ever built in the United States and the fastest liner built anywhere.

In 1948, William bought the 48,500-square-foot lot at the end of Gap Head Road on the giant rock ledge called Gap Head looking across at Straitsmouth Island. On this lot, he built a magnificent ultramodern house that was highlighted by a large deck overlooking the island in the shape of an ocean liner's bow. It was obvious that Gibbs's architectural experience was used in the design.

The Gibbs Brothers Medal, awarded by the United States National Academy of Sciences (NAS) for outstanding contributions in the field of naval architecture and marine engineering, was established by a gift from William

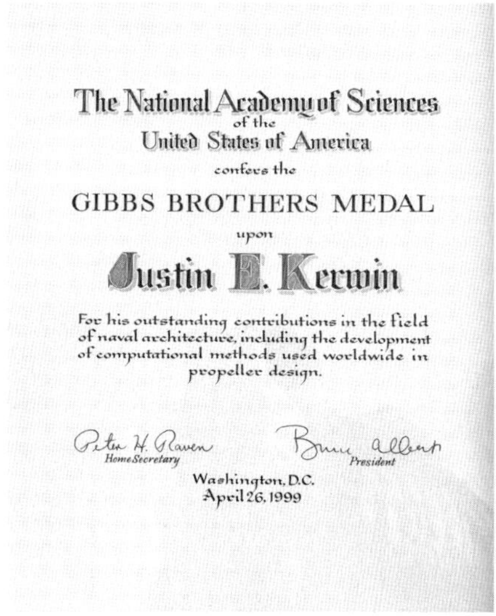

The National Academy of Sciences
of the
United States of America
confers the
GIBBS BROTHERS MEDAL
upon
Justin E. Kerwin
For his outstanding contributions in the field of naval architecture, including the development of computational methods used worldwide in propeller design.

Peter H. Raven, Home Secretary
Bruce Alberts, President
Washington, D.C.
April 26, 1999

Justin (Jake) Kerwin, *right*, is shown accepting the Gibbs Brothers Medal from President Bruce Michael Alberts of the U.S. Academy of Sciences on April 26, 1999. The accompanying scroll noted it was for "outstanding contributions in the field of naval architecture, including the development of computational methods used worldwide in propeller design." *Justin Kerwin.*

and Frederic Gibbs. William had been a longtime member of the Academy. Nominees should be individuals whose careers have been primarily focused on work in the United States. Past recipients have demonstrated a wide range of accomplishments, including contributions to naval warships, containerships, submarines, propellers, offshore platforms, classification systems and many more. The medal recipient receives $20,000, an illuminated scroll and vermeil medal and expenses to attend the presentation ceremony at the NAS Annual Meeting in Washington, D.C.

In 1999, Justin (Jake) E. Kerwin was awarded the medal "[f]or his outstanding contributions in the field of naval architecture, including the development of computational methods used worldwide in propeller design." As an interesting coincidence, Jake and Marilyn Kerwin now live on Marmion Way in view of Straitsmouth Island and William Francis Gibbs's home on Gap Head. Only eighteen medals have been awarded between 1965 and 2017.

Gibbs was awarded the Franklin Institute's Franklin Medal in 1953. He is honored at the United States Merchant Marine Academy at Kings Point, New York, in the naming of the Marine Engineering Building, Fulton-Gibbs Hall, an honor shared with Robert Fulton.

FREDERIC GIBBS, 1964–67

In January 1964, William Gibbs turned over ownership of the island to his brother, Frederic. William Gibbs died on September 6, 1967, in New York City.

MASS AUDUBON, 1967–PRESENT

Frederic Gibbs, on October 16, 1967, donated the island to Mass Audubon to be maintained as a wildlife sanctuary. The deed reads in part: "This conveyance is for the purpose of establishing and maintaining a wildlife sanctuary where plants, birds and animals may exist in their natural state… such use may include the construction of appropriate observational, interpretive and educational facilities designed to further public knowledge and appreciation of wildlife and other natural resources."

At one time in 1960, Gibbs's stepson, Adrian Larkin, went out to do work on the keeper house in the hopes of making it livable again. It had been empty since the Coast Guard first sold it in 1941. Larkin was a bachelor in his forties. He once commented on the conditions he met when he began living there in the summers for a story in the *New York Times*: "[T]he sea gulls were having their babies in the bedrooms." Larkin would drive up from New York every Friday and take up his small outboard loaded with supplies, pieces of furniture and materials needed for repairs. Each year, he built his own wooden dock, which disappeared each winter. His landing technique had him maneuvering his boat with his oar, gondola style, lassoing a boulder and drawing the boat in. He managed over the period of six years to install a shower, a flush toilet and an electric generator; refinish the floors and the chimney; repair the broken windows; repaint the inside; and do some minor decorating, including adding drapes, some Victorian rocking chairs and a small vegetable garden.

In 1983, four young men from the area offered Mass Audubon to help restore the keeper house in exchange for use of the building to live in during the summer. The house had been plagued with vandalism over the years, with no one living there since the mid-1960s. The four young men were Ted Twombly, nineteen; his brother, Peter, seventeen; and friends Peter Grammas, twenty, and Keith Gray, twenty-three. They decided to take the first step toward living on their own island. In the past, others had attempted to restore the house but had usually given up because of vandalism. Several years prior, Charles Costello, who used to fish off the island, replaced the windows in the house. But when the weather calmed, many people visited the island, and the windows were broken within days. The boys discovered that "there wasn't a window left in the place and it was filled with four-feet of bird and rat droppings. There were dead seagulls and skeletons and rats as big as cats," according to Twombly. The boys returned in the summer of 1984 to clean out the house and replace some of the windows. Local merchants donated supplies and a boat. Gene "Shorty" Lesch, the harbormaster, would occasionally check in on how the boys were doing. They were able to paint two of the seven rooms, and some rugs were laid down.

Straitsmouth Light Station was added to the National Register of Historic Places as of June 15, 1987 (no. 19870615). Obviously, there was enough public interest in this venue to make application for National Register status.

Once again, interest in the restoration of the keeper dwelling waned, and no one attempted to do any work on the island until the October 1991 "Perfect Storm" destroyed the entry cabin of the lighthouse. Because the lighthouse was still owned and operated by the Coast Guard, repairs had to be made quickly. By the following spring, a team of outside contractors and the Coast Guard cutter *Evergreen* came to rebuild the entryway door. The decision had been made not to replace the entry cabin. The following year, an outside contractor came to install a riprap breakwater in front of the lighthouse tower, designed to shear the breaking waves away from the tower. To this day, it is still intact and doing its job, and the lighthouse has not suffered any external damage since 1992. At the same time, the lighthouse was automated with a solar-powered light and foghorn.

In 1998, the Lighthouse Preservation Society (a local nonprofit organization) tried to buy the keeper house from Mass Audubon and move the house to Newburyport. Mass Audubon later denied this request after town selectmen and townspeople objected to losing this locally important historic building.

On July 11, 2008, the General Service Administration offered the lighthouse tower and 1.8 acres of land to interested parties per the U.S. Lighthouse Preservation Act of 2000. This act made hundreds of lighthouses available to local organizations and individuals who agreed to restore and maintain lighthouse properties according to a strict set of rules and regulations.

The National Register of Historic Places plaque awarded by the U.S. Department of the Interior in 1987. *Author's collection.*

The National Historic Lighthouse Preservation Act of 2000 (NHLPA) created a process for the transfer of federally owned lighthouses into private hands. It was created as an extension of the National Historic Preservation Act of 1966. Maintenance of aids to navigation had been assigned to the federal government from the beginning, first under the Department of the Treasury and called the U.S. Lighthouse Establishment and then under the U.S. Light-House Board (1852–1910) and its successor, the U.S. Lighthouse Service. In 1939, lighthouses were placed under the authority of the United States Coast Guard, which also took over the manning of lights with keepers.

Throughout this period, the expense of maintaining and staffing lights was constantly rising. Automation of lights began early in the twentieth century, and a major push in the early 1960s relieved all but a few lighthouses of their keepers. Thacher Island was automated and given over to the Town of Rockport in 1980.

Lighthouses are high-maintenance structures, being subject to marine air and the erosional effects of wave and ice. Unmanned structures were also found vulnerable to vandalism and theft. Therefore, automation of many lights led to their effective demolition.

The expense of maintaining the lighthouses continued to drag on the Coast Guard budget. On the other hand, there is much sentimental and historical attachment to lighthouses. Many surviving are listed in the National Register of Historic Places. While some lighthouses had been transferred to museums, most are impossible to move.

The NHLPA was enacted in 2000 as an amendment to the National Historic Preservation Act of 1966. Establishing ownership is a multi-step process involving United States Coast Guard, the General Services Administration (GSA) and the National Park Service (NPS).

The first step to transferring ownership is the determination of the property as "excess to service requirements" by the Coast Guard and its identification as a historic structure. This determination is reported to the GSA, and notice is given that application be made for the structure. In this phase, nonprofit and/or historical organizations may apply; if the application is made and accepted, the lighthouse is simply transferred to the applicant subject to compliance with requirements to maintain the light and make it available to the public. The NPS administers this section of the program. If no suitable applications are received, GSA may put the structure up for sale at auction.

On September 17, 2008, the National Park Service recognized the Town of Rockport and Thacher Island Association's (TIA) interest in accepting the island and forwarded instructions for application. TIA applied on behalf of the Town of Rockport for the lighthouse and 1.8 acres of land on which the lighthouse stood on October 1, 2008. On July 16, 2009, Ken Salazar, secretary of the interior, notified Town of Rockport officials that he would accept the National Park Service's recommendation to award the island to the town. GSA and USCG also approved. On September 15, 2009, the Bay Colony Group surveyed the island and placed granite markers in order to complete the deed land area specifications. In October, GSA sent the draft deed to the town for review by town attorneys.

The town's board of selectmen approved acceptance of the Straitsmouth Lighthouse and land on July 21, 2010, and the title was filed at registry of deeds.

Straitsmouth Island now has shared ownership with Mass Audubon and Rockport. The town owns 1.8 acres and the lighthouse, while Mass Audubon owns the remaining 28.0 acres, the keeper house, the oil house and a deteriorated barn. The lighthouse remains an active aid to navigation, and the light and fog signal are powered by solar panels and continue to be maintained by the Coast Guard.

The future is bright for the island because three strong organizations have partnered to manage, rehabilitate and preserve this most historical site.

Chapter 11

MODERN-DAY RESTORATION, 2010–PRESENT

In May 2010, a 3,500-pound mooring stone and buoy were placed at the north side of the island, to be used with a haul out line. This haul out line enables the TIA launch to land in a small rocky cove on the northeastern end of the island only at high tide—the same location of the derrick built there in 1901 to facilitate deliveries of materials and supplies to the light keepers and which was removed in 1970.

A licensing easement was signed in March 2011 by the town with Mass Audubon permitting an access path from the mooring landing to the lighthouse across its property.

The first major project taken on by the Thacher Island volunteers was to restore the Audubon-owned oil house built in 1905. They installed a new roof, trim and door from July to September 2011. This small six-by-twelve-foot brick building was used as a storage shed for tools and materials needed for the lighthouse restoration work planned for 2013 and beyond.

Mass Audubon wanted to give the keeper house to the town and was often quoted as saying, "Our main interest is in birds not buildings." The town, along with the advice from the TIA, was more than happy to accept the building but, before doing so, requested that Mass Audubon make the building weather tight and do some major exterior work, including on the roof, before the town would agree to accept it. The entire eastern wall had fallen off, exposing the second-floor rafters, which were open to the weather.

Audubon hired an independent contractor, Joe Roy, and delivered lumber and other materials via helicopter for the keeper house exterior stabilization project, which began on October 1, 2011. In the summer of 2012, a new contractor, Napco Corporation, took over to add a new roof, clapboard siding, trim and a new chimney, as well as to frame in new windows. A series of cleats and eye bolts were drilled into the ledge on north side inlet to enable the launch to tie up for island access of workers. By the end of 2013, the contractor, with help of TIA volunteers, had completed the stabilization, adding lightning arrestors, new porches and final painting.

TIA began a fundraising program in 2011 and raised $150,000 to complete the stabilization and repair of the lighthouse tower. International Chimney Corporation was contracted to add steel support beams inside for the upper platform beneath the lantern room, repoint brickwork on interior column lining and external pointing, paint all metal work and exterior and repair the entry door.

A trail was cut from the house to the western end at Gap Cove, where the future boat ramp was to be built. This trail provided another access point for the Thacher work boats to dispatch the volunteer parties. The distance from the Gap Cove location to the keeper house is about one-third of a mile.

In 2014, the town was informed by Mass Audubon that it was unable to give the keeper house to the town after all. According to the instructions given by the Gibbs family in their bequest, any of the structures on the island had to be sold at full market value and could not be given away. Rockport then countered with an alternative plan whereby the town would agree to a long-term thirty-year lease for one dollar a year. Mass Audubon happily agreed, and the Rockport town meeting voted to approve a renewable lease for the keeper house and oil house.

The plan was to someday install resident summer keepers on the island, as had been done on Thacher some twenty-five years earlier. In the summer of 2019, TIA began the keeper house interior restoration to make it habitable for keepers to live there for the first time in eighty-five years.

Trail clearing continued in the summer of 2015. Boulders were split or moved to allow tractor access. Installation of live motion-sensor web cams for security purposes were installed on the oil house and on the lighthouse and barn. The house cisterns were cleaned out to prepare them for use in 2017. The only source of water from 1835 to the present day is from rainwater runoff from the roof of the keeper house into two three-thousand-gallon brick cisterns located in an attached shed.

Planning started in 2016 for the creation of a 120-foot boat ramp on western shore at the Gap. This was the same location that the U.S.

Keeper House before restoration, 2010. *Author's collection.*

Keeper House after restoration, 2019. *Author's collection.*

Lighthouse Service had built the original boat ramp and a boathouse in 1860. All were destroyed and abandoned in 1934. Although a distance away from the keeper house, it is the area on the island most protected from severe northeast storms. Plans were revised to a shorter 105-by-12-foot ramp. Thus began a long and frustrating series of permitting, licensing and board approvals. Because this ramp would be built on the coastal bank, a variety of permits were required by the state, local and federal agencies. Conservation Commissions, DEP and Army Corps of Engineers had several environmental requirements to be met. Special engineering drawings were created, and engineering inspections had to be completed. It took more than three years to accomplish all the requirements.

In the meantime, the volunteers put their efforts toward building a sixteen-by-twenty-four-foot maintenance and storage barn. By this time, the work crew was being referred to as the "Straitsmouth Savages" because of its tenacity to land on the rocky ledges covered with slippery seaweed and clambering over the rocks at any tide, carrying tools and materials needed for the day's work, fighting poison ivy, dealing with ticks, the sun and many times the rain on an island with little or no shade.

During this period, the TIA established a successful campaign to raise more than $400,000 to complete this important access point for both the volunteers and the public for years to come. Grants, donations, fundraising events and memberships all contributed to financing this project.

Keeper house restoration was essentially 90 percent complete in 2017; the only remaining projects were the final kitchen cabinets installation, finished plumbing, activation of the solar electric power system and water filter system, all of which were completed in the spring of 2018.

Boat launch ramp bids were sent out in the winter of 2018, and the project was awarded to a local marine construction company that agreed to do the job for $397,000. Ramp construction was started in August and completed in November 2018.

At the same time, the keeper house restoration was completed, as was the storage/workshop barn. Period furniture and household goods had been collected from many donors in the area. The idea was to create a Victorian period parlor in the keeper dwelling that could be used as a visitor center and exhibit room, with nautical artifacts and island memorabilia.

The island no longer depends on electric power from the cable from the mainland now deemed unusable. In its place, a solar power system was designed with eight solar panels (photovoltaic modules) on the south-facing roof of barn and solar control room in the house, which include inverters, a

New boat landing ramp, 2019. *Author's collection.*

New kitchen in the Keeper House, 2019. *Author's collection.*

control module and twelve deep cell storage batteries in case of cloudy days. This system now powers the entire island, with additional panels erected at the ramp end and backup generators in place near the house and barn.

During the summer of 2018, the footbridge walkway area was cleared of poison ivy, and the original thirty-two granite pilings that supported the original footbridge were found. Most of the granite pilings were intact, although a few needed repairs. The summers of 2019 and 2020 saw the reemergence of the footbridge, missing since 1910.

An appraisal assessment by the Town of Rockport valued the island at $1,997,200, including the buildings.

The boat winch and hydraulic motor were installed on the ramp and are used to tow up the two Thacher launch boats. A winch motor house was constructed on bluff above the ramp, and the winch (capstan) was bolted to a concrete block on the bluff. Solar panels and equipment installed on the bluff provide electric power for a marine radio, security web cam and other electrical needs at this end of the island.

Adjacent to the ramp, a deck was built to accommodate kayakers, who are required to remove their kayaks from the ramp itself to allow the Thacher launches to land.

As was done on Thacher in 2015, a composting toilet (privy) was built across the trail from the winch motor shed for the public's use. This toilet is powered with solar panels to activate the composting system as well as a fan and a light inside.

Directional, interpretive and memorial signage was designed and installed in cooperation with Mass Audubon, including a large "Welcome to Straitsmouth" sign with a directional map located near the landing ramp. Memorial plaques were established to recognize the contributions made by Rockport residents through the Community Preservation Act and private funding by the Manton Foundation.

The Thacher Island Association has invested more than $750,000 since beginning work on Straitsmouth in 2010 to preserve the historic infrastructure.

The first resident keepers began living there in June 2019, and a group of twenty-five keepers was scheduled weekly to manage the island until September.

In 2019, the island was opened to public for first time in 184 years. From 1835, when the first federally operated lighthouse was established, to 2019, members of the public were not allowed on the island. From 1835 until 1933, it was federal property under the management of the U.S. Lighthouse

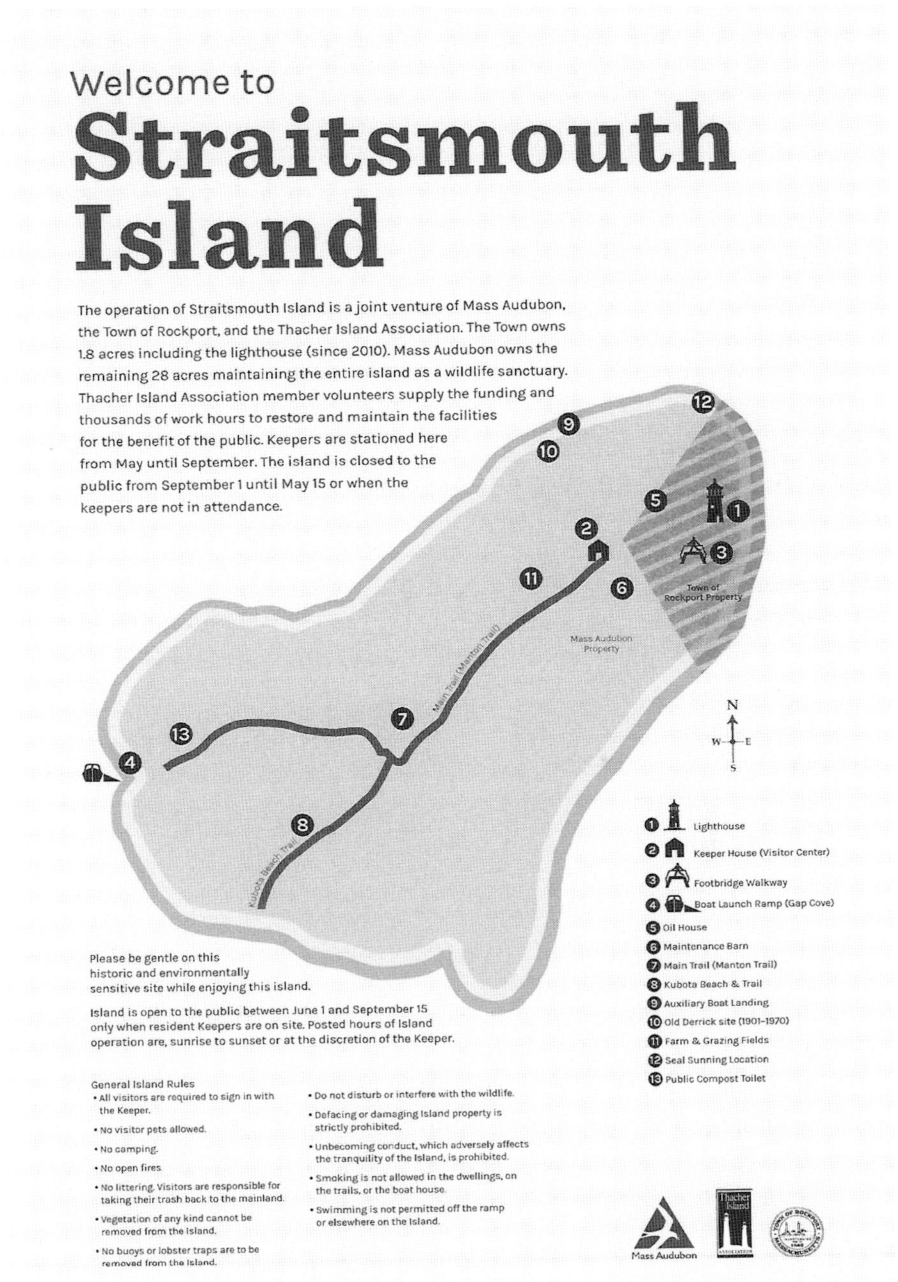

Welcome sign to Straitsmouth Island. *Author's collection.*

Establishment, then the U.S. Lighthouse Service and finally the U.S. Coast Guard. Starting in 1941, it was privately owned, and the public was again denied access. Even though when Mass Audubon was given the island in 1967 to maintain it as a wildlife sanctuary, it had certain restrictions to public access because there was no safe means to land. Finally, in 2010, the Thacher Island Association, the Town of Rockport and Mass Audubon joined in a collaborative effort to make the island accessible to everyone as both a historic site and a wildlife sanctuary. Today, it is home to hundreds of bird species, a family of wild turkeys, deer and gray and harbor seals.

The lighthouse remains an official aid to navigation operated by the Coast Guard and owned by the Town of Rockport. Its solar-powered green light flashes every six seconds, and a fog signal watches over the entrance to Rockport Harbor today, just as it has done since 1835.

Go to the Thacher Island website to see more information, photographs and videos about Straitsmouth Island (www.thacherisland.org).

BIBLIOGRAPHY

Babson, John J. *History of the Town of Gloucester, Cape Ann, including the Town of Rockport.* Gloucester, MA: Proctor Brothers, 1860.

Babson, Roger W., and Foster Saville. *Cape Ann: A Tourist Guide.* Rockport, MA: Cape Ann Old Book Shop, 1936, 1945.

Bates, Raymond H., Jr. *Shipwrecks North of Boston.* Vol. 2, *Cape Ann.* Charleston, SC: CreateSpace, 2016.

Beal, Clifford. *Quelch's Gold.* Washington, D.C.: Potomac Books, 2008.

Cann, Donald, and John Galluzzo. *The Coast Guard in Massachusetts.* Charleston, SC: Arcadia Publishing, 2011.

Cape Ann Light Station, Thachers Island. National Register Nomination Form, October 7, 1971.

Champlain, Samuel de. *Voyages of Samuel de Champlain, 1604–1618.* New York: American Historical Association, Charles Scribner Sons, June 1907.

Claflin, James. *Lighthouses and Life Saving along the Massachusetts Coast.* Charleston, SC: Arcadia Publishing, 1998.

Copeland, Melvin T., and Elliott C. Rogers. *Saga of Cape Ann.* Freeport, ME: Bond Wheelwright Company, 1960.

D'Entremont, Jeremy. *Lighthouses of Massachusetts.* Boston: Commonwealth Press, 2008.

Dolin, Eric Jay. *Black Flags, Blue Waters.* New York: W.W. Norton and Company, 2018.

Erkkila, Barbara. *Hammers on Stone.* Woolrich, ME: TBW Books, 1980.

Garland, Joseph. *Guns off Gloucester.* Gloucester, MA: Essex County Newspapers Inc., 1975.

Garland, Joseph E. *Down to the Sea.* Boston: David R. Godine, 1983.

———. *The Gloucester Guide: A Stroll through Place and Time.* Rockport, MA: Protean Press, 1990.

Gleason, Sarah C. *Kindly Lights.* Boston: Beacon Press, 1991.

Gott, Lemuel. *History of Rockport.* Rockport, ME: Rockport Review Press, 1888.

Greenbaum, Dan. *Ten Pound Island: A Closer Look.* Gloucester, MA: Resources for Cape Ann, 1975.

Grimes, George. *Water Under the Keel: Memoirs of a Sea Going Life.* Rockland: Milk Island Press, Maine Publishing, 2011.

Hill, Benjamin D., and Winfield S. Nevins. *The North Shore of Massachusetts Bay.* 4th ed. Salem, MA: Illustrated Guide, 1881.

Holland, Francis Ross. *America's Lighthouses.* New York: Dover Publications, 1988.

Kenny, Herbert A. *Cape Ann: Cape America.* Gloucester, MA: Curious Traveler Press, 1971.

Lepionka, Mary Ellen. "Native Americans of Cape Ann." Historic Ipswich, February–August 2018. historicipswich.org.

———. Survey of "Indian Relics" for the Sandy Bay Historical Society, December 12, 2012–January 25, 2013. Files available at historical society.

———. Unpublished papers on Cape Ann prehistory. *Bulletin of the Massachusetts Archaeological Society* 74 (Fall 2013).

Lewis, Winslow. *Description of the Lighthouses on the Coast of the United States.* Boston: Thomas Bangs, 1817.

McIntire, E.C. *Picturesque Cape Ann.* Gloucester, ME, 1910.

Morison, Samuel Eliot. *The Maritime History of Massachusetts, 1783–1860.* Boston: Northeastern University Press, 1979.

Morris, John N. *Alone at Sea: Gloucester in the Age of the Dorymen, 1623–1939.* Beverly, MA: Commonwealth Editions, 2010.

Parsons, Eleanor C. *Thachers: Island of the Twin Lights.* Canaan, NH: Phoenix Publishing, 1985.

Pool, Ebenezer. *Pool Papers.* Vols. 1–5. Sandy Bay Historical Society, 1823.

Pringle, James R. *History of the Town and City of Gloucester, Cape Ann, Massachusetts*, 1892.

Robinson, F.J.G. *Tragabigzana or Cape Ann.* Boston: Progressive Print, 1935.

Shaler, N.S. *Geology of Cape Ann.* Washington D.C., 1889.

Smith, John. *A Description of New England, 1616.* 3rd series. Boston: Massachusetts Historical Society, 1837.

Snow, Edward Rowe. *Famous Lighthouses of New England*. Boston: Yankee Publishing, 1945.

Solley, George Willis. *Alluring Rockport*. Rockport, ME, 1924.

St. Germain, Paul. Cape Ann Light Station, Thacher Island. National Historic Landmark Nomination Form, 1999.

———. *Lighthouses and Lifesaving Stations on Cape Ann*. Charleston, SC: Arcadia Publishing, 2013.

———. *Sandy Bay Harbor of Refuge and the Navy*. Charleston, SC: Arcadia Publishing, 2018.

Swan, Marshall W.S. *Town on Sandy Bay*. Canaan, NH: Phoenix Publishing, 1980.

Thacher's Woe and Avery's Fall. Gloucester, MA: Press Room, 1985.

U.S. Light-House Board. *Annual Reports of the U.S. Light-House Board*. Washington, D.C.: 1852–1939 Government Printing Office.

U.S. Lighthouse Service Clippings Files. National Archives, Washington, D.C., 1855–1932.

Walen, Harry I. *The Role of Thacher's Island in the American Revolution*. Reprinted from the *Bulletin of the Order of the Founders & Patriots of America* (Spring 1985).

INDEX

F

G

H

I

K

L

M

N

O

P

ABOUT THE AUTHOR

Paul St. Germain has been a resident of Rockport, Massachusetts, for the past twenty-five years. His interest in the Cape Ann area began in 1999, when he was asked to join the Thacher Island Association's board of directors, eventually being elected president in 2002. In 2000, he researched and wrote the successful nomination application resulting in the designation of the Cape Ann Light Station on Thacher Island as a National Historic Landmark by the Interior Department's National Park Service. He has written four books in Arcadia Publishing's Images of America series: *Sandy Bay National Harbor of Refuge and the Navy*, *Cape Ann Granite*, *Lighthouses and Lifesaving Stations on Cape Ann* and *Twin Lights of Thacher Island.*

A graduate of Boston University and a recipient of a master's degree from Northeastern University, he has held several senior-level marketing and advertising positions of major international athletic footwear and soft drink manufacturers.

St. Germain is also a board member of the Sandy Bay Historical Society as well as the Thacher Island Association. When he's not focusing on fundraising efforts for the preservation of structures on both Thacher and Straitsmouth Islands, he volunteers during the summer months to do carpentry work on both coastal islands.

Saving Straitsmouth Island: A History traces Straitsmouth Island beginning one thousand years ago, when Indians spent summers there, to the completion of the restoration of its historic structures in 2020. He has worked on this project with association volunteers for the past nine years, resulting in the island being opened to the public for the first time in 180 years. His book is the first complete history of the island, documenting its 300 years as a significant historic maritime site. This is his first work for The History Press.